GAME IT UP!

Library Technology Essentials

About the Series

The *Library Technology Essentials* series helps librarians utilize today's hottest new technologies as well as ready themselves for tomorrow's. The series features titles that cover the A–Z of how to leverage the latest and most cutting-edge technologies and trends to deliver new library services.

Today's forward-thinking libraries are responding to changes in information consumption, new technological advancements, and growing user expectations by devising groundbreaking ways to remain relevant in a rapidly changing digital world. This collection of primers guides libraries along the path to innovation through step-by-step instruction. Written by the field's top experts, these handbooks serve as the ultimate gateway to the newest and most promising emerging technology trends. Filled with practical advice and projects for libraries to implement right now, these books inspire readers to start leveraging these new techniques and tools today.

About the Series Editor

Ellyssa Kroski is the Director of Information Technology at the New York Law Institute as well as an award-winning editor and author of 22 books including *Law Librarianship in the Digital Age* for which she won the AALL's 2014 Joseph L. Andrews Legal Literature Award. Her ten-book technology series, The Tech Set, won the ALA's Best Book in Library Literature Award in 2011. She is a librarian, an adjunct faculty member at Pratt Institute, and an international conference speaker. She speaks at several conferences a year, mainly about new tech trends, digital strategy, and libraries.

Titles in the Series

GAME IT UP!

Using Gamification to Incentivize Your Library

David Folmar

ROWMAN & LITTLEFIELD
Lanham • Boulder • New York • London

Published by Rowman & Littlefield
A wholly owned subsidiary of The Rowman & Littlefield Publishing Group,
Inc.
4501 Forbes Boulevard, Suite 200, Lanham, Maryland 20706
www.rowman.com

Unit A, Whitacre Mews, 26-34 Stannary Street, London SE11 4AB

British Library Cataloguing in Publication Information Available

Library of Congress Cataloging-in-Publication Data

Folmar, David, 1969-
Game it up! : using gamification to incentivize your library / David Folmar.
pages cm – (Library technology essentials ; volume 7)
Includes bibliographical references and index.
ISBN 978-1-4422-5334-6 (cloth : alk. paper) – ISBN 978-1-4422-5335-3 (pbk. : alk. paper) – ISBN
978-1-4422-5336-0 (ebook)
1. Libraries and community. 2. Libraries–Social aspects. 3. Libraries–Marketing. 4. Library orientation. 5. Game theory. 6. Incentive (Psychology) 7. Games–Social aspects. 8. Games–Design and
construction. I. Title.
Z716.4.F65 2015
021.2–dc23
2015011703

Printed in the United States of America

CONTENTS

SERIES EDITOR'S FOREWORD

Incorporating the principles of game thinking into everyday tasks and workflows has become a steadily growing practice among businesses and libraries alike who hope to incentivize their staff and patrons. In *Game it Up! Using Gamification to Incentivize Your Library*, expert author David Folmar instructs readers about the ins and outs of setting up a gamification program in your library. This start-to-finish primer examines the building blocks of these programs, such as game thinking, game elements, player types, gamification platforms, and game design software, and goes on to lead the reader through how to gamify everything from staff orientation to patron services. Readers are guided through the process of planning and implementing projects such as how to gamify information literacy education using interactive fiction, how to create leaderboards and gamify programs with badges, how to gamify your library's collection using augmented reality to link it to your library, and even how to build your own library video game in this ultimate guidebook!

The idea for the Library Technology Essentials book series came about because there have been many drastic changes in information consumption, new technological advancements, and growing user expectations over the past few years, which forward-thinking libraries are responding to by devising groundbreaking ways to remain relevant in a rapidly changing digital world. I saw a need for a practical set of guidebooks that libraries could use to inform themselves about how to stay on the cutting edge by implementing new programs, services, and technologies to match their patrons' expectations.

Libraries today are embracing new and emerging technologies, transforming themselves into community hubs and places of co-creation through makerspaces, developing information commons spaces, and even taking on new roles and formats, all the while searching for ways to decrease budget lines, add value, and prove the return on investment of the library. The Library Technology Essentials series is a collection of primers to guide libraries along the path to innovation through step-by-step instruction. Written by the field's top experts, these handbooks are meant to serve as the ultimate gateway to the newest and most promising emerging technology trends. Filled with practical advice and project ideas for libraries to implement right now, these books will hopefully inspire readers to start leveraging these new techniques and tools today.

Each book follows the same format and outline, guiding the reader through the A to Z of how to leverage the latest and most cutting-edge technologies and trends to deliver new library services. The "Projects" chapter constitutes the largest portion of the books, providing library initiatives that can be implemented by both beginner and advanced readers and accommodating for all audiences and levels of technical expertise. These projects and programs range from the basic "How to Circulate Wearable Technology in Your Library," and "How to Host a FIRST Robotics Team at the Library" to intermediate such as "How to Create a Hands-Free Digital Exhibit Showcase with Microsoft Kinect," to the more advanced options such as "Implementing a Scalable E-Resources Management System" and "How to Gamify Library Orientation for Patrons with a Top-Down Video Game." Readers of all skill levels will find something of interest in these books.

David Folmar spoke at the Computers in Libraries 2014 conference about "Gamification for Community Engagement" in libraries. As soon as I saw his presentation, I knew that he needed to write the book in the series on gamification. Not only were his ideas forward-thinking and innovative, he had practical experience using gamification to promote library services in his position as the emerging technology librarian at the Richmond Public Library. David took his firsthand experience and pioneering ideas and filled this book with outstanding projects and ad-

vice. If you're contemplating how you might gamify your library processes, you'll want to consult this book.

Ellyssa Kroski

Director of Information Technology

The New York Law Institute

http://www.ellyssakroski.com

http://ccgclibraries.com

ellyssakroski@yahoo.com

PREFACE

Games, games, games. What is the obsession with video games? They are fun. It is as simple as that. Personally, I still love to play video games. I run programs in my library, playing with teens and tweens. The fun part is that sometimes the parents play too. I have seen daughters, mothers, and grandmothers all playing the same game and laughing together. I know that people have problems with games, video or otherwise. There is always the one person who thinks that something has to be hard and painful to be worthwhile, but sometimes people need to have fun as well. So our main objective will be to make things fun. There is more detail in the book about how fun is really about working and by playing a game we *are* learning. But if the game is not fun, then it doesn't work, and fun is really what gamification is about.

The first two chapters look at what gamification is and will give you an overview of what it really means and explain how gamifying is a process. The next chapter details the available tools and how they might be used to add game concepts and theories to library processes. Chapter 4 discusses the many ways that libraries are starting to explore gamification and serious games in the context of their organizations. The bulk of the book is found in the "Projects" chapter, which will walk readers through the steps to implement gamification in their organizations. Individually, the projects can be used to promote your library. Together, they can be the basis of an ongoing gamification of your services. The final chapters discuss best practices and helpful advice for how you can further explore your own attempts at gamification as well as what's on the horizon in this evolving field.

I hope this book will give a good start when you follow the projects, but also I hope that it inspires you to create projects of your own. Customization is the key to gamification. In the end, it is really about listening to our patrons and meeting them where they are in terms of technology and self-expression. When gamification fails, it is because it wasn't fun.

ACKNOWLEDGMENTS

I, of course, thank everybody. In this case I especially thank my wife, Lorraine, because you should thank your wife. I thank the TI-99/4A; it knows why. Thank you to my daughter, Ellie; my son, Augie; friend Jim Greco; and the kids in Richmond Public Library's LAN gaming program—for my love of video games and keeping me "in the loop" in gaming. Thank you to RVA GameJams, Will Blanton, and Laura Vercelli especially; and to Dr. Ryan Patton of VCU CurrentLabs and Phillip McMinn of Euchonic Games for helping me explore game creation for fun and basic media or coding literacy. Thank you to librarians Mary Broussard and Eli Neiburger for taking time to talk of their work, and Patricia Parks who is an encouraging if sometimes confusing boss. A special thanks goes to Ingrid Callenberger for being my reader and first proofer. Finally, thank you to Ellyssa Kroski for this opportunity.

1

AN INTRODUCTION TO GAMIFICATION

SO YOU WANT TO TRY GAMIFICATION

Gamification is the process of using game theory to inform an activity or incentivize participants. There is a surplus of exciting ways you can use gamification in your library, such as motivating staff, bringing patrons into the library, driving traffic to your website, and more. This book will discuss a variety of ways you can easily leverage gamification in your library to successfully engage your community.

Gamification is growing rapidly in popularity. Companies, school systems, and numerous online applications have introduced some elements of gamification to improve engagement with employees, students, and the general public. It has been widely repeated by supporters of gamification that "over 70 percent of Forbes Global 2000 companies surveyed in 2013 said they planned to use Gamification for the purposes of marketing and customer retention."[1] So why would they decide to use gamification? In large part, it is because of video games. Schools use gamification because it is a type of digital language that students understand. Video games have been in existence more than fifty years now, which has led people to think about ways that they can utilize these elements of game design to motivate people in new ways. Badging, points, and leaderboards, three of the main staples of gamification, all represent a form of feedback that millennials are both familiar with and respond to, and each is borrowed from video games.

Video games are played by 58 percent of Americans, whose average age is thirty, and there is a balanced mix of both male and female gamers. Actually, there are now more females over the age of thirty playing video games than boys under eighteen, and over one-third of parents play games with their kids regularly.

Marketers and software developers have taken the tools and methods used in developing video games, the most explosive entertainment sector in the United States, and applied them to other activities. Activities such as getting a team to sell more, encouraging people to shop at a store, or motivating people to learn are all types of gamification—and now, in the case of libraries, how to inform patrons about new services, encourage patron use of resources, or motivate staff to make their facilities better and more effective. The reason to try gamification is because of its promise to help engage your patrons in a novel way, to hopefully increase the use of your services. To that end, let's talk about what gamification really is beyond the tools we use to express it.

WHAT IS GAMIFICATION?

The most commonly used definition for gamification is "the use of game mechanics for non-game ends." However, a better definition is "gamification is the use of *game thinking* and game mechanics" to meet non-game ends. And yet, while it is increasingly common for people to design an online experience that has some level of gamification, those experiences are not always designed with *game thinking* used to produce the outcome. Templates often used in online gamification are the many elements of video games such as badges, leaderboards, and point systems.

These elements are familiar to players in online video games. Badges are awards for accomplishments given to the player in the form of an image representing an achievement. They are used both inside the games for accomplishments and shared from games to gaming services like Microsoft Live, PlayStation Network, and Steam. This sharing not only made networks more popular, but it also made the games themselves more popular inside the chosen network.

Zynga, the popular game maker, most famous for *Farmville*, partnered with Facebook to host games, a relationship that both served

Zynga and made Facebook more popular, providing different content to increase visits to Facebook and allowing gamers to capitalize on their social connections for game benefits. Also, apps like Foursquare, the app for checking into restaurants and shops, gamify leisure time and shopping by rewarding its users for how and where they spend their time. This has helped gamification to gain interest. In response to this trend, marketers jumped on board with their own versions of gamification to sell their products and services. Now, rewards are built into online banking as well as credit cards; spending earns users points and allows them to redeem money spent in different categories by giving customers a coupon for similar services at other retailers.

The books in this series focus on using technology. When we think of technology we think of it as computer- or machine-based. While much of gamification in based on computer applications and applications built for making games, it is only half the technology behind gamification. There is another aspect to gamification, and understanding it will be what makes your projects either fail or succeed.

Gaming is cross-generational, and in 2012, people spent $14.8 billion on video games,[2] which is $4 billion more than they spent going to movies. All that money spent, you'd think somebody was figuring out how to make games better and more attractive to people. And they have. Game design has grown from a few maverick engineers and programmers to a specialization, including people who look only at the psychology of what makes people play and keep playing and refine tools for this purpose. Technology is an applied science, and the other non-digital science gamification is based on is behavioral science.

GAMES AS LEARNING TOOLS

When we talk about gamification, we usually think of and see it expressed digitally in badges, point systems, and leaderboards, referred to by people studying this as BPL. While BPL has it uses, it is important to understand the context in which it is effective. Without that, it is a rather limited view of what gamification is or can be. BPL elements are the easiest to understand in relationship to a call center or checking out a book. BPL has been around for a long time and is easily understood by people who participate in gamification. Boy Scouts use badges; leaderboards are used in sports and also for sales jobs, so these are familiar elements.

In school, grades are a kind of point system. Even the idea of rewarding behaviors in commercial and financial endeavors like banking and credit cards is not terribly novel, especially to those of us who remember S&H Green Stamps, which was a sort of badging system with rewards for shopping.

The part of gamification that seems to have captured the attention of people is its use with new technology like social sharing. It has added to its effectiveness, but the core of how gamification can truly be used effectively is not by keeping track of existing processes but encouraging new ones.

In the book *For the Win*, the authors describe three benefits of Gamification[3]:

- internal: a way for an organization to increase production (e.g., leaderboards for sales forces);
- external: using games to improve relationships between organizations and their users (e.g., Microsoft Live badges for achievements or Foursquare naming you the mayor);
- behavior-change gamification: when you use games as a means to introduce new behaviors, in effect, encouraging the player to internalize a value system the designer is promoting (e.g., some of us really wanted that high GPA; we knew a *C* would let us pass, but took pride in an *A*).

We really want to achieve the third goal of gamification. The first two aspects will appeal to you as a stakeholder—improved performance and improved relations—but they are dependent on achieving the third. I discuss the psychology aspect of gameplay throughout the book because if you introduce the first and second without the third, your success will be very limited.

Behavior change is the real power of gamification. A library, like any organization, needs to have efficient and motivated workers. It also needs patrons, clients, and customers, whichever term you like, engaged with your mission. To make behavioral changes in an organization, a superficial understanding of gamification can be more of a hindrance than help.

SERIOUS GAMES

To better understand behavioral-change gamification, it is important to look at "serious games." These are short-term activities meant to teach a lesson or achieve a nongame goal within the framework of a game, for example, the "Reader Rabbit" series that uses a game to teach children reading. It is a game with a completion stage as compared to gamification, which is meant to create ongoing and prolonged engagement. If you want to know more about serious games, you can read Jane McGonigal's *Reality Is Broken*, which is a great work into how "games" can be used to engage and teach while driven by a sense of social commitment.[4] Some of the projects in this book are closer to serious games.

The idea of serious games is not new. Chess, for instance, has been used as a learning tool for centuries. It is a serious game in respect to developing military strategy. Monopoly, invented by Elizabeth (Lizzie) J. Maggie Phillips, was intended as an educational tool to illustrate the negative aspects of concentrating land in private monopolies. It was intended to illustrate the fact that renting was a bad idea. Game thinking requires us to understand where the pleasure of winning is, how the *act* of playing is teaching the lesson, and how the *act* of winning reinforces the lesson that you were meant to learn. But when you play Monopoly the pleasure of winning is in bankrupting the other players, not in ensuring that everyone has a place to live by the end of the game. The fact that the victory conditions of the popular version of the game she invented is exactly what she was trying to educate against is one of those sad ironies of history. It also can be used to illustrate what makes gamification different from serious games.

Gamification is not just making a game, which imparts a lesson; it is applying *game thinking* to how we impart that lesson and continuing to develop it based on the feedback of the players. We live in a time when game thinking is more studied and hopefully better understood than ever. Video games, connecting with a player's ability to provide input from the Internet, have made a fantastic feedback loop. Game designers regularly refine and expand gameplay based on the input of their players. It has not been the digitization of mechanics that have allowed game designers to fine-tune "what works and what doesn't"; it has been the speed and growth of direct feedback from communities of players.

FLOW AND WORK VS. PLAY

So you are going to become a game designer? Congratulations! What that means is that you will want to consider how games actually "work" and what will make your player "work" at winning! What I mean by "work" is that you will want to look at out how games impart a lesson; learning the mechanics of a game is an important step in that direction. You will understand that better by reading this book. You will understand how Monopoly is disconnected from its original purpose by its own design. Monopoly was a serious game that showed the value of a "single tax on land value," and we all still get that from the game. No, we don't; we play to own everything and bankrupt everyone else. The original intention of Monopoly is lost to the majority of users. If there had been a way to tweak gameplay, Monopoly could have continued to fulfill its original intent. Of course, Parker Brothers may not have been too interested in that, but in any case, it does not serve the inventor's original intention. It is a game about controlling the board because that is where players derived pleasure in the play and in that way it thrived.

I suggest Monopoly as it illustrates what drives play and how we gain meaning from it. The first person to address this academically was Mihaly Csikszentmihalyi, in his work *Flow*.[5] He wanted to know what made people lose themselves in an activity. He stated that the joy of play is not from winning or in fulfilling an objective. To illustrate Csikszentmihalyi's work, let's take a look at golf. How does one win at golf? 1. Get the ball in the hole. 2. Beat your opponent. However, how do you get that ball into the hole? If I just wanted to fulfill the objective, I would pick up my ball and go and drop it into the hole. Instead though, people use a ridiculously small ball and small hole and hit the ball with a variety of specialized sticks, over fairly large distances. It seems like a lot of trouble to get a little ball in a little hole.

In a rather large nutshell, Csikszentmihalyi said, "Work is not the opposite of play but for play to be interesting it requires work." We play games because the challenge is interesting. The reward for playing games is overcoming an obstacle as well as winning the game. It is why many don't enjoy playing a game against an uneven opponent or why we don't just go drop the ball in the hole in golf. It is also why video games come with different levels of difficulty. To be fun, a game has to be hard; we need to feel like a win was "earned."

Returning to gamification, we cannot simply reward people for what they would do anyhow. It is nice, but it is not a game. There must be continuing levels of difficulty to earn the reward in order to maintain engagement. It is through overcoming this difficulty that enjoyment of play is derived. To make a game meaningful, you will also need the challenges to impart a lesson and make it meaningful. If the challenge of Monopoly is to own all the properties on the whole board, that is what people do and that is the lesson it teaches you, to own all the land. You need to reward them for both the challenge of the game and learning the lesson. It is easier than it sounds; most of it has to do with breaking the game into multiple objectives and rewarding the player for each one.

MORE THAN BADGES, POINTS, AND LEADERBOARDS— THINK LIKE A GAME DESIGNER

Badges and points can be awarded to everyone who participates in an activity and are a great start to a gamified process. Most libraries will have a summer reading program that gives a list of books. Whether they read them all or not, the patrons will get a certificate or a prize. The BPL can be used to generate a progress bar that will show how well someone is doing on completing his or her reading list. Some libraries will use a prize to encourage everyone to finish, but often there aren't enough prizes to give to everyone who finishes.

A prize is nice, but accessing the next level or moving to the next book becomes a reward in itself. More importantly perhaps, those who work hard and cannot finish all of the books or who are not randomly selected to win the prize do not feel like their effort was wasted. You have five prizes and forty people finish the summer reading list; what message does this send the thirty-five who are not selected? You may have forty finishers who completed the work, but only five feel like winners. In a gamified system, the idea is that effort is rewarded, with badges or points, even when the objective is not completed. That is what gamification does; it rewards the effort, not the winning.

Do not assume that just using BPL will make an interesting game. Some players will not respond to it. If the nonresponsive audience is whom you want to reach, you need to find other means. People think adding BPL to their activity log can do miraculous things. It can, but it can also reinforce behaviors you're trying to teach.

What do the players know and what don't they know?
What do the players do, and what don't they do?
What can they do, and what can't they do?
Keep developing the game to challenge them!

Flow can be created if you know your audience. Be fun; start somewhere a player can succeed. They need to feel goals are attainable. Increase difficulty and rewards based on the players' achievements.

The first concern should not be about the resources or the message, but about the player having fun. You can make the player feel that it was worth using Dewey Decimal or LOC to look up a book or worth attending a program. The elements of gameplay—narrative and mechanics—can make this happen by creating a challenge in the game, and rewarding it in a meaningful way.

Kevin Werbach of the University of Pennsylvania has this advice to offer: "always think of them as a player first" when talking about gamification. This is the best advice that I've heard on the matter. Gamification efforts fail because the best intentions cannot make a game fun; it will always have to be a good game first. Use or modify the projects in this book and think about the patrons as players, because that is what they are. Remember to keep it fun, in gamification and life.

NOTES

1. Jennifer Van Grove, "Gamification: How Competition Is Reinventing Business, Marketing & Everyday Life," Mashable, July 28, 2011, http://mashable.com/2011/07/28/gamification/ (retrieved February 12, 2013).

2. The NPD Group/Retail Tracking Service; Games Market Dynamics: U.S.

3. Kevin Werbach and Dan Hunter, *For the Win: How Game Thinking Can Revolutionize Your Business* (Philadelphia: Wharton Digital, 2012).

4. Jane McGonigal, *Reality Is Broken: Why Games Make Us Better and How They Can Change the World* (New York: Penguin, 2011).

5. Mihaly Csikszentmihalyi, *Flow: The Psychology of Optimal Experience* (New York: Harper & Row, 1990).

2

GETTING STARTED WITH GAMIFICATION

You might be a little intimidated by creating a game. Don't be: the idea of gamifying an activity is not new. Did your mom or a teacher ever tell you when you got bored of doing a chore, like peeling a potato, "to make a little game of it"? It is an easy way to get people to do something and actually have fun doing it. So you're basically using the same approach moms, teachers, and nannies have used for decades if not centuries.

So why the term *gamification*? Why are people interested in this now, and how does it differ from what has come before? One large part is the tools, like the badges, points, and leaderboards expressed in digital form. The BPL is what we see used most often in gamification or when people are designing a game for educational and promotional purposes. These are just game elements though; even now that we can award them digitally and share them across social networks, the more interesting aspect of gamification is how and why they are awarded. What is new about gamification? It is the sophistication of the approach to making a game out of activities. Rewards have a diminishing return the more often they are given. So how we give the awards, whatever the form—praise, badges, or points—is only part of what we need to understand. We also need to think of contexts in which rewards are given in games. Gamification is not just about new types of game elements used to reward behaviors but also the structures of escalating rewards and about how you need to reward people in meaningful ways. A term for this approach to design is game thinking.

GAME THINKING

My mother's potato-peeling game, for example, will work for a time. By seeing who could peel the most potatoes for dinner, she could get us to engage with an otherwise boring chore. There comes a point where children will figure out the returning thrill of "being the best potato peeler in the kitchen" is not worth the effort. To parents' credit everywhere, in the process, the child usually developed skill at peeling potatoes, a good idea for how long it *should* take to peel potatoes, and hopefully a bit of a work ethic. So was this gamification? Yes, it was. Was it a good gamification? Well, that depended on the parent and whether the child developed the work ethic. The point of the "potato-peeling game" is not really about "peeling potatoes"; it is about contributing and working for family. If the children drop out because they did not feel appropriately compensated for their effort, they cannot go on to learn the bigger lesson.

So how do you stop the child from dropping out? A clever game designer would use game thinking to reward not just the child who peels the most potatoes but also the one who does it the cleanest or the one who shows the other child how to do it better—offering new challenges and rewards for the same activity, as can be approached differently by different children and their skills. The overall point of introducing you to game thinking is thinking like a game designer. By nature you have to use game elements, but you also need to tailor them to your audience to keep them engaged.

WHAT KINDS OF PEOPLE PLAY GAMES? *EVERYONE...*

When you think of your design, try and ask yourself what the player will get from the game. Will the game test the players' skill sets in a way they are interested in and try to encourage new ones? Also, you need to remember that games and gamers are not a monolithic type. You can design a better game if you understand these three points:

1. The average concept of a game player is the adolescent male, sitting around killing things on a screen in isolation. I mentioned the 2013 study that showed the average age of gamers is thirty, only 32 percent are under eighteen, and 45 percent of all gamers are female. In fact there are more women over thirty who are gamers than boys under eighteen, and over 50 percent of parents play games with their children.

2. The types of play and players are not limited to common stereotypes. One of the projects in chapter 5 will be more of a contest than a game, which will illustrate that much of gamification encourages not just the game itself, but the concept of *play*. And thinking about different types of players will help you break away from the idea that there is only one way to play, and only one way to reward a player.

3. Although we are all going to be thinking like designers now, the premise of our systems is as an education and marketing tool; we want to appeal to the largest audience possible. We need to think about how we can encourage all the player types to interact with the game and make any social-sharing element appeal to players no matter how they play. The social part of gamification is the most important part for promotion. Not only does this help us promote the library, but prestige is a large part of what people play for.

"GOOD NEWS, EVERYONE": YOU'RE GOING TO BE A GAME DESIGNER!

The first thing you need to think about is *how* to design a good game. Fittingly for librarians, you start off with a good story. One of the people talking about how to design a good game is Matt Allmer. He wrote a well-received blog post on game design called "The 13 Basic Principles of Gameplay" for Gamasutra.[1] It is based on, or perhaps more aptly described as a reimagining of, Pixar's classic "22 Rules of Storytelling." Some of these rules translate into ways to engage with game audiences. We can take advantage of these works and their insight into the way game elements can be used to make a good game.

If had to pick a point, from both Allmer's and Pixar's lists, that is the most basic rule you need to know, it is number 2: "Write for your audience not for yourself." It is a good way to think, especially as you may not be a game player yourself. Or maybe you are a hardcore gamer and you have two platform systems, and you love *Call of Duty: Black Ops*, but don't understand why you keep getting *FarmVille* requests, with its slow pace and boring graphics. Or worse yet, you may have to explain this project to people who do not understand or appreciate games and game playing.

Whatever the case, you're designing for your patrons and how they play. When we cover player types, realize that all of them are in your library. If you can design a better game for them, it will be more effective for your institution. Then you can put something in the game for them and understand how it appeals to those players.

BARTLE'S FOUR PLAYER TYPES

We talked about the concept of "flow" and how it applies to games and learned that game designers are basically behavioral scientists in a limited application. It should not be too surprising that behavioral scientists have also become interested in game design. Perhaps one of the most well-known works in the field of game design is by Richard Bartle. He has been involved with creating multi-user games since the late 1970s. In his book *Designing Virtual Worlds*, he introduced four player types: achievers, explorers, socializers, and killers.[2] He has expanded his theories from the original four to include eight player types. However, I am going to refer to the original four player types he described because the takeaway from this is different types engage with gameplay for different reasons.

Bartle postulates that players exist on an x/y axis of acting/interacting and players/world, and please remember they are positions on a scale, not absolutes.

TYPES OF PLAYERS

Killer: A killer measures success by outdoing specific other players. The killer wants to have a higher score, more badges, and so on. Making a team is a good idea for this kind of player; it can focus their efforts. To the killer, the actual accomplishment is only useful when it is relation to others.

Achiever: An achiever wants to be first. If you give them a selection of badges, they will attempt to collect them all because their pleasure arises from the accomplishment of mastering the system.

Socializer: A socializer's motivation is to influence others. Ironically, we often think of killers and achievers when we think of games, but games would not be possible without socializers. Pictionary or Twister are games for socializers. *FarmVille* is a digital social game. If you're using points, let the socializers award

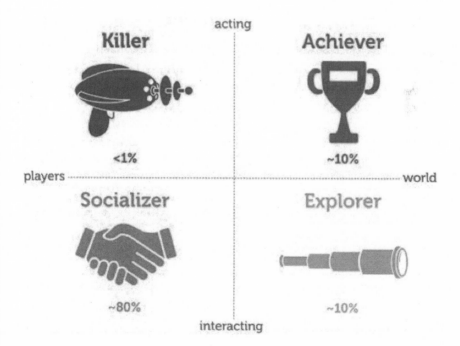

Figure 2.1. Courtesy of *Gamification at Work* by Janaki Kumar and Mario Herger. Creative Commons Attribution-NoDerivs 3.0 Unported.

badges and points. Socializers derive pleasure from influencing other players.

Explorer: Outside of the game, these would probably be the kinds of people who come to the library anyhow because of a natural thirst for knowing things. Explorers love the sense of discovery. In a gamification system, you might want to hide some special bonuses, points, or knowledge inside the game.

IDENTIFYING YOUR PLAYER

Functionally, you need to be designing for all four player types in a true gamification system. Inside the projects scope of this book, I had to limit the types of players that were rewarded by each game because I included multiple projects. However, once you understand what motivates a player type, you can come up with your own ideas of how a game should be designed or modified. Here is where your game elements will be helpful. When we think about games, we usually only address the needs of the first two types of users, killers and achievers. These are traditionally how we view games, as competitive sport. The BPL is actually primarily for these people, but really it must be used in conjunction with a public-facing aspect for a reason.

- Killers use badges and points in the context of a leaderboard, the more public a leaderboard the better. If you can include a way for killers to socially advertise they are beating an opponent, either directly to that opponent or in a wider context, they will feel rewarded.
- Achievers use badges and points to keep track of their achievement. More importantly, you must let them know how much of the possible rewards or objectives they have reached. Achievers will not be happy until they have achieved all of them. A progress bar is a good tool for achievers.
- Socializers need to communicate that they are helping or interacting with other players. If you let them give a hint on how they won a badge or comment on an achievement or more importantly award an achievement themselves, their needs are met.

- Explorers will also like to give hints and they will like to see the badges, but their objectives, not being competitive, need to be self-directed. For instance, if you use the passport game (discussed in the projects section), include a special badge for people who visit all the branches inside a week. Or include some other sort of unexpected reward, which by sharing or seeing that it has been shared will give them impetus to explore more.

The social aspects of the game give the competitive parts a platform for the achievements to mean something. More importantly, I think social elements have perhaps the more interesting applications in creating community, and that success can be shared outside the library. Social sharing will give you a way you can reach a new player, including those who do not regularly visit your library. It becomes a key element not only for the social player types but also in making the gamification effective as a tool for community engagement.

So when you create a game, think of your four player types. Ask yourself what about this game will appeal to them. Do you have something for achievers, killers, socializers, and explorers? In what way can you build something in it for them?

Word of Warning

While some games can focus on certain types of players, it is important not to exclude the others. A well-designed gamification system should try to meet the needs of all of the four player types. In this way you will reach the widest possible audience.

Questions people might ask:

- Why not just make a game for explorers? They are how we typify library users anyhow.
- Why not focus on accommodating the socializers so they can spread the word? This is meant to be promotional.
- Why do we want competitors? Players should realize learning is a reward in itself.
- Why do we need to find ways to reward a "killer" type?

You can respond with the obvious answer that all types of players should have library services. But also, the idea behind making games for everyone's style of play is because whatever the goal of a game, people will always play it in their own style and adapt the game accordingly. So it makes sense to reward each player's style.

Let me digress with a story about the fantasy series Ultima. It has a somewhat complex ethical code that the players were intended to follow. "Lord British," an avatar of the game's creator, supposedly embodied the code. He roamed the land doling out help to players throughout the series and was mostly invincible. It is the "mostly" that is important here. When Origin, the company that made the franchise, introduced *Ultima Online* in 1997, one of the first massively multiplayer online role-playing games (MMORPGs), Lord British made an appearance and was promptly killed. Hence the *Lord British Postulate*: "If it exists as a living creature in an MMORPG, someone, somewhere, will try to kill it." The point of that story was that even though Ultima built in a higher code, there will always be a player who will look to play the game not in the way you want, but the way they want. Don't fight this trend; know this and accommodate all the kinds of players.

GAME ELEMENTS

To start designing a game, you need to understand all the elements and how they reinforce each other. The easiest and broadest distinctions you can make are: *narrative* and *mechanics*. When you go into creating a gamified system of any type, after you have identified what you want to promote as a librarian or marketer for the library, you have identified the goals you wish to promote and make part of your *narrative*. In this sense I simply mean *narrative* as *"a series of obstacles to master."*[3]

> Example: The player gets points for checking out books to become the King of Readers, or the player's avatar finds every resource on the map of the library branch, making them win the game.

I would like to point out here that my use of the word *narrative* is somewhat loose; I don't mean it as a plot or story or even narrative, but a hybrid of all three. What I am describing as *narrative* is comparatively easy. It is the information, resources, or programs you're trying to promote. You create a narrative by making learning these obstacles of your games. Then make that discovery or utilization of those resources the path to mastery. To create this narrative, and to make it meaningful, is when you will be using game *mechanics*.

Yes, good game design can tell a story too; story can give context to the choices the player makes. A good story is also a nice launching point for interest in the games. Many of the other points Allmer makes in his blog post "The 13 Basic Principles of Gameplay" are about characters and more traditional story elements. An example of the effectiveness of story in a game is Mario, one of the most popular video game characters of all time. He first appeared in the arcade game *Donkey Kong* in 1981. *Donkey Kong*'s game mechanics were not really superior in any way to contemporary games like *Pac-Man*, *Burger Time*, or *Space Invaders*. However, somehow the story of a plumber saving a princess from a barrel-throwing ape caught the popular attention in a different way.

If you are looking to make a patron understand Dewey, you don't engage them by saying figure out the Dewy Decimal system and win a badge. I suppose some people are interested in knowing more about how books are cataloged, but I doubt that the number is as large as the number of people who will be interested in playing a game called "Zombies in the Library," which is a project in this book about understanding information literacy. I enjoy the zombie apocalypse meme, but I am not suggesting it is going to work for you. Figuring out your story is another part of figuring out your audience. Whatever story you make, it will have some element that could be used to justify the *mechanics*.

There is one thing I need to stress: the game *narrative* needs to be reinforced by the game *mechanics*. We are still using the tools of gamification for a purpose. The mechanics of the game are to make people think about something differently. Again, this is the "serious" or "meaningful" games framework that is the foundation of the study of games for more than amusement. "Serious games" help people re-evaluate what they know and hopefully learn something new.

Story and narrative are always part of a game structure. Most games teach an inevitable lesson. Chess is a great example: on one level it is a strategy game; on another level it tells about medieval power structures. Pawns are expendable; lose the king and you lose the game. He is the least mobile or powerful piece on the board. It is important that you consider the game mechanics as well as the goals and how they reinforce each other in the mind of the player. While we want to introduce a resource in a fun, creative way, we also want to help people understand the value of that resource.

Let us look at mechanics in games and see why they are important in gamification and what that means to our game design. We are going to look at Monopoly. When Elizabeth "Lizzie" J. Phillips invented "the Landlord's Game" or Monopoly, as it evolved into, she seemed to have the same idea of how to use games to create awareness or give meaning as serious games do today. It was designed to teach about why monopolies were bad. But did she understand her audience and how they would interpret it? The players receive pleasure from the game by gaining a monopoly.

The problem with Monopoly seems that the challenge of playing was the direct opposite of the lesson to learn. The challenge was to own everything. Therefore, whether Ms. Phillips intended it or not, she made a game that rewarded people for the very behaviors she was trying to dissuade instead of reinforcing the idea that it was illustrating as it was originally intended. (It seems like she needed to have heard of the *Lord British Postulate*, because people ended up playing Monopoly as killers, not socializers.)

When you are considering the gamification projects in chapter 5, it will be helpful to keep that in mind. Game mechanics need to reward the right decision. If you were to play Monopoly and add an element where everyone you bankrupted made you responsible to pay when they landed on a property, or all your property had an upkeep cost relative to the value of the property, what would that game look like? You wouldn't want to bankrupt anyone, at least not at first, and you wouldn't want to buy up Park Place and Boardwalk until you had other properties. It might encourage slow, steady growth and preserving the others players for their purchasing power, over grabbing high-value properties right away. Those are two very different modes of play, and they impart two very different lessons.

When you develop a game, remember the fun of playing is the reward as much as the badges are. In essence, the playing is the point, not the winning. In true gamification there are no "win" conditions; instead, the pleasure and lesson come from mastering the challenges and a steady increase in difficulty and reward. If you can identify the player's area of pleasure in the process of achieving your objective, there is the area you need to reinforce, not winning. In this way we are imparting the third objective of gamification, which is behavior modification and to change thinking.

Of course, for that to be successful you need to reward your audience for the right reasons and still make a good game. No matter how noble or important what you're trying to teach is to someone, it will not reach the audience you intend unless you achieve in making it fun. An easy mistake is making the game easy to win and thinking the players understand the lesson based on their participation instead of their engagement. Think again at how I hacked Monopoly: that aspect of changing things is really what sets gamification apart from serious games.

FEEDBACK LOOPS

If the idea of designing good games and changing your games to make them better seems a little overwhelming, it is not. It is a series of small steps, and the best part is that the players want to help you. The projects will be a good start, but you may tailor them for your library's audience. And that's actually very easy, if you pay attention to the players. Addressing and balancing the needs of different player types may seem intimidating when you are trying to think of all the player types at once. However, they are individuals, and those distinctions are somewhat blurry when applied in real life. We don't need to start out by making a huge gamified project. We can start with some serious games and focus on certain player types and game mechanics that work for that type. Then watch how the game is used and adjust accordingly.

A term for this is *game balance*. Basically, it is the application of flow in a challenge/reward relationship. A game must achieve a balance between being challenging enough to hold your interest and easy enough to play without being frustrating. That balance will change over time as players leave and join the game. What adjustments do you make? You base them on how the game is played and the players' likes and dislikes. Do you know what their likes and dislikes are? Of course not; you can make educated guesses, but you couldn't possibly know starting out.

A useful example is *World of Warcraft*. Some people have played the game for more than ten years, and at its height, in 2010, the game had twelve million players. It has only stayed as popular as it is by changing. Those changes were driven by how people played the game and gave their direct feedback. MMORPGs like *World of Warcraft* are the basis of a lot of gamification theory.

In essence, *game balance* means that when a game doesn't work, you can adjust it to work better. Making a game work better for your audience is like making "house rules." In some houses, the fines paid in Monopoly are claimed for landing on free parking, but not in others. The rule does even the field a little by adding a larger element of chance to the outcome. When I play with these rules, the game is longer and there is a better chance of less-experienced players winning. Is this why people added the rule? I do not know. However, it seems very possible and does suggest that there was a feedback loop to make the game more even. Changes are part of gameplay, and people want balanced games.

Failing Forward

Be prepared to do it. Failure is an option; it should, in fact, be an expectation. There is no way I could design a game that would be perfect for *your* patrons any more than I could send you a perfect collection policy. So deal with designing a game the same way you deal with creating collection policies: accept suggestions, watch how things are used, and change according to feedback. Game developers make a series of games, and they usually try and make them better based on what they were told by the players. We are actually in a much better position: our games or gamification have all those developers' research and efforts to learn from.

There are concepts from software development that I could refer to as well: agile development or user experience (UX) specialization. In a nutshell, these IT concepts work under one premise: be willing to change and always make room in your system for change based on the use. Look at what you're doing well, look at what you're doing badly, and then either capitalize on it or correct it because mistakes are part of the process.

Keeping Open Channels

If you look back at traditional game development, the jumps and the effort in understanding why games work in the past two decades are substantial. Gamers have communities on the Internet. Board games and traditional sports always had people talking about them, but the process for designers answering those questions was relatively limited. Now with video games, message boards, online chats, and e-mail, designers get feedback on *exactly* what works and what doesn't.

Those communities can hold large ongoing discussions that exist in an easy repository for game publishers to research. This data is not just interesting from a marketing viewpoint but from a social science viewpoint; you suddenly see a huge amount of raw data available for study. Video games in combination with the Internet have proven to be a great lab for adjusting games to players' styles. It has allowed drawing some more interesting conclusions about gameplay. We are able to see that tweaking the mechanics can prolong engagement, and that if you let a culture grow around a game, the game is more effective in reaching an audience.

Many of the projects in this book rely on websites, some on blogging platforms like WordPress. They are useful for letting players share tips or brag about achievements, which is part of the pleasure derived for social players. In the context of feedback, they are also great resources for listening to players and adjusting the game. Some important tips to using the Web for feedback:

- Create a message board for feedback and moderate the forums so you can keep track of responses.
- Web pages offer analytics: how often a page is viewed over time, how many return versus unique visits. These statistics are a great way of judging user behavior. Adjust your game by watching how many people play and how people play.
- Make changes and see how people respond.
- Respond to your players' comments. If they say something is lame, ask what is fun and not fun. Did you get bored? What bored you?
- Ask questions. It lets them know you are engaged with their play.

For the player, questions will help improve a game if they are acted upon, but the important part is asking questions. Even if the players don't see their changes built into a game, it makes them feel valued. Even better, if their suggestions are acted upon, it gives them a sense of ownership of the game. In a sense, they helped design it.

Design your game with room to grow based on their suggestions and you increase your players' sense of ownership, which makes a better player community. Of course, not all suggestions will be able to be acted upon. Some changes may even be derided by your players, but that is okay; be prepared to do the wrong thing. Doing the wrong thing might not be as bad as doing nothing. Let me explain why this is true.

One of the strongest arguments for trying gamification is that you will be creating a feedback loop between patrons and your library. I stated that gamification creates a new bridge for social engagement between staff and your patrons, one that uses tools and methods the public has already adopted in gaming and social networks. Remember, this is not about kids sitting staring silently at computers, or even marketing the library; it is about games as a means to engage the community.

In the end it will be social engagement that creates the best chance at promotion of the library. If we have social engagement, can we perhaps reinforce positive social engagement? A game like *World of Warcraft* makes teamwork and collaboration necessary to unlock all of its abilities. The killer and achiever need to interact socially to achieve their goals. In a sense, they are forced to be a different kind of player until they accept these conditions as necessary to become the kind of player they are naturally inclined to be. As I mentioned, there is a large body of work on what makes a good video game, and I have distilled as best I can, but remember to look to your patrons; you will find something that can help you.

Library processes can be gamified, in a meaningful way, without large-scale structures, money, and skill sets to support it. You can start small too. Your system will not be perfect, but we can reward behaviors that benefit our organizations. It is possible to promote programs and increase engagement with the community through gamifying the basic processes we have. If we then use the socializing aspect of gamification, we are letting our patrons know we care about what they are doing.

SOCIAL ENGAGEMENT

Let me start by sharing an anecdote from a workshop on game design I attended at Virginia Commonwealth University CurrentLab. We were looking at programs to teach video games as part of art education. Dr. Ryan Patton approaches them as an artistic expression, and we broke into groups and played several games in succession trying to decipher what made a challenging game and what didn't. While I tried to view the games as a series of mechanics and what was challenging and what wasn't, I discussed it with the two art teachers I was paired with. When we were done, we were asked to say what our impressions of the game were.

While the others talked about a design being challenging or too complex, my initial thought was about what I learned from the others about who they were, where they went to school, how they liked to spend their time. It was not technically part of the game design, but the act of shared gaming gives people a common ground to express themselves. Play is inherently social; even when it is pitting you against someone, it is still an interaction. When you think of the solitary gamer, remember that she or he may be alone in a room, but it still gives that person a shared experience by which to connect with others.

Social media is something every business and institution is trying to capitalize on these days. However, like many things in gamification, it serves a dual purpose. We can use our social sharing not only to enhance gameplay and create a venue for players to measure their success, but it also helps to promote our library services.

Let me explain. This is a simplified version of a social networking, with your page at the center. In this case:

- Light gray is your library.
- Medium gray is your reach across social networks.
- Black is people connected to your reach but not connected to the library.

If you put out notices about programs, you will reach those who are attached to your social presence.

When someone shares, they include their circle of friends and their attention to your site. Awarding a badge works the same way. If you add

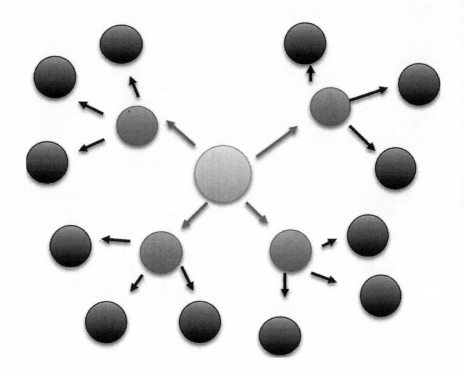

Figure 2.2.

an element on your site to promote their achievements in library gamified systems, you add players to each other's circle of attention. So now they are aware of not just the library but of other patron users. They may find that the other players use the library differently; maybe it will be something they didn't know was going on, like a class or workshop. Not only are they interested in competing for points, but they also have discovered new ways to use the library.

The Web as the platform for gamification not only creates awareness of your library, but the uses others in the community make of it. This dual purpose is not driven by institutional self-interest; social game players need to measure their success not by points but rather by how well it reaches their peers. It can also create new peers, new connections in the community. The rules for social engagement are:

- Whenever possible, it's beneficial to add a social element to a game.

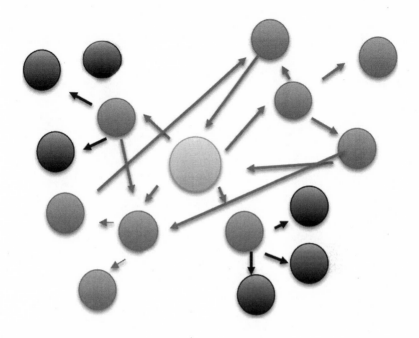

Figure 2.3.

- Create this social element in the form of a bragging right to make others interested in achieving.
- Use your platform as an area for players to discover each other and grow new connections.

PERMA, Making Engagement Positive

We also need to use social engagement responsibly. Libraries try to proactively make the community better. We need to think of how people engage with each other. There is a movement in video game design called "ethical gaming," related to "serious gaming." Their objective is to make games for the greater good. While I don't want to limit your creativity, this may be something that you'll want to consider, and it aligns with the goals of libraries fairly well. In the projects chapter, you'll note that I didn't create a first-person shooter in a gamified library. This is due in part to the fact that the mechanics of shooting and aiming do not teach library processes, but also due to the subtext of that lesson. In the same way, our mechanics can impart positive lessons if we consider how we use the narrative elements and how social engagement can positively affect our community.

Dr. Martin Segelman of the University of Pennsylvania brings this concept to gamification from the emerging field of positive psychology; it is called PERMA.[4] Positive psychology looks to ways to increase happiness rather than deal with mental illness. So PERMA, at least in this limited context, can be a good guide for what we want a gamified system to offer. Many game designers have adopted it as a framework for a positive "game life" experience.

Looking at PERMA, you will see some familiar concepts from good game design when we break the acronym down.

> P: positive emotions
> E: engagement
> R: positive relationships
> M: meaning
> A: accomplishment

In a macro sense, you could just say that for gamification to be engaging and valid, it also needs to be a positive experience, that afterward the players feel like they have achieved something or that they are better for having played it.

FINAL NOTE

As a final note to this chapter, I'd like to mention one last thing about engagement. We don't need to only develop gamification systems that address engaging patrons with information inside our library. I feel that we can use these tools to also help promote the growth of skill sets and information literacy inside our community. In effect, we can use games and game systems for everything that a library has traditionally done with books. So when you think of how to use these projects, and hopefully create your own, don't think merely in terms of our existing processes. While we can gamify our own processes, we can also gamify the objectives of those processes: information, education, and our community.

The reason to use gamification is engagement; it is a kind of language that is spoken and a framework that is understood by many people, some of whom may not be regular users of the library. Rather than just using it to validate and promote what a library does, also think about how games can be used by libraries to do new things for the community and serve our patrons.

Returning to the question of whether we can really make a gamified system with the complexity I describe, the answer is it might be easier than you think! Luckily, the indie game developer movement is growing, and some of the tools you will use in this book are made to let people take control of this burgeoning trend for themselves. There is an active groundswell of people constructing games and sharing information on how to make them, as well as more theoretical and critical work available than ever before.

NOTES

1. http://www.gamasutra.com/view/feature/3949/the_13_basic_principles_of_.php.

2. Richard A. Bartle, *Designing Virtual Worlds* (Berkeley, CA: New Riders, 2004).

3. 3 However, like the traditional idea of narrative, it should not be closed or have too fixed a structure. We don't need to have five acts in a game.

4. Martin E. P. Seligman, *Flourish: A Visionary New Understanding of Happiness and Well-Being* (New York: Free, 2011).

3

TOOLS AND APPLICATIONS

PREEXISTING GAMIFICATION PLATFORMS

What can you do with the existing gamification platforms? While many of today's platforms are limited in both what they can do and the audience they are built for, creative marketers (and librarians!) can find a way to use them to their advantage.

Badgeville or BunchBall

Currently, BunchBall and Badgeville are the 800-pound gorillas in the field of gamification. They are each gamification platforms for the enterprise. Similar to most of the other preexisting gamification platforms, they are primarily constructed for businesses and are not ideal for non-profit organizations. They reward brand loyalty and motivate customer relations and sales force improvement. These types of services tend to be priced as software as a service (SaaS), which means that subscribing to their services is not likely to fit the library budget. Also, they seem to be prominently geared to monetary or coupon rewards, which don't have a clear application with library usage. This is not meant to suggest that gamification platforms may not move in the direction of nonprofit engagement in the future, just that none have yet.

Aside from the budget considerations, to create something that works in a library context, these systems would need significant cooperation between integrated library system (ILS) providers and the gamification platforms. While it's true no "formal" gamification system has arisen in the ILS world, library vendors have been open to accepting elements such as "LibraryThing" integration, which brings elements of social sharing to your catalog. This makes it seem inevitable that one of the major players will eventually find a way to exploit the nonprofit market. Much of what the major players do will depend on the success of the gamification system created specifically for libraries. The only "off the shelf" option that now exists is a UK product called Librarygame.

Librarygame

At the time of this writing, there does exist one gamification platform that was developed specifically for libraries called Librarygame. According to its website:

> Librarygame is a bespoke library enhancement product that adds game elements directly into the library experience to make it more fun, engaging and delightful. As well as giving your library patrons a fresh social discovery interface, Librarygame also provides useful metrics on how your library is being used.

Librarygame is not widely distributed; however, versions are being developed by the University of Glasgow and the University of Manchester in the UK. It is primarily focused, unsurprisingly, on academic libraries. Also, the software development partner, Running in the Halls Inc., has a version available for public libraries called Orangetree. As of now, there are no disclosed partners or users of Orangetree.

The problem I see with the Librarygame is twofold:

1. While it is still in development and promises the gamification of book checkouts and database usage, there seems to be little application beyond that.
2. The company customizes the software for your library. While customization is a necessary part of gamification, the idea of outsourcing it to a software development team seems like an expensive option.

Librarygame at best seems a half measure. I feel like the feasibility of gamification of book checkouts will depend a great deal on the enterprise ILS systems that become involved. Most ILSs are moving toward providing software as a service themselves over the next few years, so it will be interesting to see if they introduce gamification elements of their own. Additionally, the social aspects that Librarygame has developed are not very different from LibraryThing (that is Library*Thing*, the reader advisory social platform, not Library*game*), and as it already has some integration with ILSs and OPACs, a small BPL system would be a logical next step. The biggest problem I see are the processes not addressed by Librarygame, such as programs, classes, or workshops, as well as community events or happenings outside the library. The existence of Librarygame is encouraging, but right now its applications are limited.

Open Badges

Open Badges is an open-source Mozilla project created to issue, display, and verify badges from multiple organizations and for a variety of achievements. It is customizable for different organizations and their needs; it allows the user to share their accomplishments either inside their own circles or through partner hosting sites. Open Badges is currently a series of hosted APIs (application programming interfaces), which means that you would need to have web development talent on your staff or available for you to make use of it. However, Mozilla is working on an open-source hosted version that would have an interface, called BadgeKit.org, currently in closed beta.

The benefit to Open Badges is still considerable. The ALA YA (Young Adult) committee is planning on using Open Badges in summer reading programs. There are existing badge-issuing sites and products that integrate with it. It is open source, and if you can host it yourself, it is a cheaper solution than the software as a service applications previously mentioned. Most importantly, since the badge development community and badge issuing community go beyond your organization, it should lead to a larger user community, which will promote your services with not simply your existing users but all Open Badges users. It could be a framework for cooperation between the library and other nonprofits in your area.

There are quite a few issuer services available now and some new ones in beta as of this writing:

1. The free version of Credly.com is discussed in the projects chapter. It could be more comprehensive, but it's stable as of this writing. Other than having free features, another nice feature to Credly is that is has WordPress and social network integration in the Pro (pay) features, which may make them worth the cost.

2. BadgeOS.org is a popular plug-in for WordPress integration. In fact, there are integration tools for every major content management system (CMS) at the moment and some minor ones. There is an Open Badge issuer in open beta at the moment you can try too, called Open Badge Factory. There is also the possibility to host your own issuer site.

3. BadgeKit.org is Mozilla's project for badge issuing without hosting your own APIs or any real development or coding skills. Unfortunately, it is in closed beta, but it will probably be of interest to many of you when it opens, as I suspect it will be one of the better-developed free sites.

INCORPORATION INTO CMS OR WEB PAGES OR SOCIAL MEDIA

One of the major aspects of gamification is social sharing; the major example I will use is the Facebook API. There are APIs for all the major and minor social networks, Twitter, Pinterest, and Blogger. I choose the Facebook API because Facebook, like it or not, is the *major* social networking site. It has the broadest appeal to the widest range of demographics, Those of you focusing on young adult or college-age groups may want to consider Twitter instead of or in addition to Facebook. I would also suggest looking at Mashable's breakdowns of social network usage by age group and demographic. http://mashable.com/2013/04/12/social-media-demographic-breakdown/.

Facebook API

A general list of the APIs can be found at https://developers.facebook. com/docs/. The one you will most likely be using is the "share" or the "like" button. More advanced users can post content using any of the options. In the projects chapter I will point you to the link to the easiest pages and the settings for how you can have patrons "like" your games on Facebook. In this way you can include a social element for your games, and use Facebook as an existing platform to do so. While many other social networks offer similar APIs, I am using Facebook since it is currently the dominant social network; however, there are other options.

Social Liking Plug-ins

When you are using WordPress, Drupal, Joomla, or another CMS, each offers a system of introducing code for social sharing that uses a much simpler interface than actually inserting all the different APIs for different social networks. The number available and how much functionality they have depend on which CMS you are using. WordPress is easily the most popular CMS in the United States. There are multiple social sharing options for WordPress in the form of widgets and plug-ins. (For more on how to use these elements of WordPress, see also the book in this series, *WordPress for Libraries* by Chad Haefele.) They can be found here: https://wordpress.org/plugins.

Drupal is very popular with many libraries that control their own websites. Unlike WordPress, Drupal requires more knowledge of actual coding and layout. If, however, you are using such a system currently, you will find share-button widgets available for it as well. They can be found here at: https://www.drupal.org/download.

Joomla is not as popular as the other two options but straddles the line between WordPress's ease of use and Drupal's customizability. It has quite a number of social sharing options and some gamification elements in what it calls the extensions. They can be found at http:// extensions.joomla.org/extensions/social-web.

One of your options in both WordPress and Joomla is to include voting options that could be incorporated in the gamifying patron engagement project. There are also more extensions and plug-ins coming out every day. If you use a CMS, it is worth looking to see if there is a plug-in that will enhance a game.

AVATAR GENERATORS

Avatars are other simple elements of gamification. They are simply online representations of players based partially on the player's physical characteristics. The appeal of avatars is that they can be whatever the player feels best represents him or her. Especially in the case of under-age patrons, it can serve to protect their identity as a privileged class. It is of benefit to older patrons with privacy concerns since they will not be disclosing any identifiable information unless they choose to. There are many avatar generators online such as Gravatar (https://en.gravatar.com/). If you choose to use one, be careful about conditions of use since often the free version has limitations to its use.

As a general overview of how they work, you are given a generic human (or sometimes another shape) and add the elements you like—hair, clothes, and so on. When the person feels he or she has something representational, he or she can save it and later access it through e-mail or by downloading the file to add it to your project. Here is a small selection of the tools I like with a brief description of each:

- Appealing to youth-oriented audiences, FaceYourManga will allow one free avatar generation per e-mail account. It straddles a car-toony feel with realistic elements, customizable for gender, eth-nicity, and body type.
- PickAFace.net is more photo realistic and may appeal to older audi-ences. It still has some elements of cartoons but with a cleaner, vector-type graphic style. It is also realistically customizable for gender, ethnicity, and body.
- DoppelMe.com's main benefit is it makes a full-figure image (as compared to a chest-up image). It is very similar in style to Face-MyManga, more limited in character style but with other options, including adding elements to backgrounds.
- Gaia Online is a social network, but it will allow you to download an avatar once created. The real fun here is that animals are one of the possibilities to use to create an avatar.

https://sites.google.com/site/webtoolsbox/avatars has a large selection of avatar generators, including human, animal, and robot.
Easily one of the most fun options, it is more kid-friendly than
others. Be careful: there are some trademarked characters here,
which while the generator seems to have permission to use them,
I am not sure how those permissions would be acceptable in your
game.

8biticon.com is probably my favorite one. While it has fewer options
than some of the others, it creates an eight-bit character pixel art.

There are still more options out there. If you use them, you can offer a
series of choices to choose from, or even use nonrepresentational art for
an avatar. A simple Google search will show many available for pur-
chase and some free ones as well, listed under Creative Commons
licenses. Some of the CMS systems have avatar plug-ins.

In my experience, staff sometimes are self-conscious about images of
themselves for whatever reason, and an avatar is an easy way to make
people who would otherwise not want their image shared more accepting of the idea. If you want to use pictures, you can as well. If you need
to combine both concerns and you need an avatar that is more recognizable than an avatar generator will allow, it is also possible to take some
pictures and apply Photoshop filters.

BADGE DESIGNERS

Badge generators allow you to create customized badges online for
sharing and rewards. To create a badge with customizable content and
sharable and traceable certification, you will need to use systems such
as Open Badges. To create a badge without the code, you don't need a
generator; you can just download an icon font and add some text to a
shape you create in applications as simple as Microsoft Word.

If you need help designing the graphic of a badge, there are online
interfaces for creating a badge for achievements in your game.

- Open Badges Designer Mozilla is easily the best of the three.
  Open Badges Generator is an online tool with fonts, colors, and
  graphics. The Open Badges Designer is an element of the larger

Open Badges project. Make sure to specify "designer" when you're looking for it at https://www.openbadges.me/.

- Webestools has some great generators for many things including badges. The badges it can create have fairly limited options but are customizable and free. http://www.webestools.com/web20-badge-generator-free-image-beta-photoshop-web20-badge-generator.html.
- 3D Badges makes the best looking of the three sites. Still not outside of the realm of anything a graphic artist can do, but it would look slicker than one generated in Word. It is very customizable and offers a variety of shapes. http://www.onlinebadgemaker.com/3d-badge-maker.

GAME DESIGN SOFTWARE

Two of the projects in this book will discuss how to create your own video game. One is a project based on a type of game called interactive fiction. The software I chose is Twine. However, there are other applications available that will enable you to create an interactive fiction game as well.

- Twine is a simple interface using a very limited coding syntax and standard HTML elements, for creating interactive fiction. The use of HTML also allows for customization. Twine is fairly straightforward and very similar to straight HTML.
- Inform has a more complex interface; however, it allows for something more like the traditional RPG text adventures from the early 1980s. If for some reason you thought to try a game combining the two projects I gave you, Inform would be a good choice.
- Adrift is another option for interactive fiction. It claims to be less code-oriented than Twine. I do not think that Twine is very code-oriented, but you may feel differently. I would point out that while it does not ask you to code, it is a more complex process to create the mechanics of the games.

The other project involves creating a graphically driven video game. For that, I chose GameMaker. GameMaker is a game program with widespread support and customizable mechanics. It has both a drag-and-drop interface and a more complex pseudo language.

Some of the other options for creating games without code are:

- Construct2
- Stencyl
- Arcade Game Studio

None of these programs allows for the same level of customization that GameMaker does. If you would like to make a more simple point-and-shoot game or side-scroller and have your own ideas how that would fit into gamification of your library, they are available options for you. If you would like to try something as complex as GameMaker allows and are still interested in trying another game design software, I would suggest trying ClickStream Fusion. ClickStream Fusion is for creating the same kind of games, but it allows for some things like free app download, which GameMaker does not, and has a free artwork library.

I would suggest that you take the time to explore the tools I gave you here. Especially take time to explore the gamification system and game design software. The other resources are shortcuts for content creation. The gamification systems will give you a working idea of how all the elements of a gamified system can be incorporated to reinforce each other. You can also see how people are using them currently and identify how the projects can be incorporated into larger gamification programs. The game design software is good for you to see how easy creating games has gotten in the past few years.

4

CASE STUDIES

In this chapter we will look at some successful attempts at gamification and the use of serious games in the library. The first two examples are about the use of serious games to promote library services, and the second two examples are about the use of gamification in libraries.

LYCOMING COLLEGE

Various academic libraries have used learning games for information literacy for the past eight years. Mary Broussard of Lycoming College has tried various models and created different games to try and "gamify" the library processes at the college library.

The Problem

Broussard explained that an introductory composition/English class is required at Lycoming College. The instructors have different approaches to teaching about information literacy, and it was not required to include an information literacy component in their courses as some other programs required. Without a formal requirement, she approached the idea of using games as a "spoonful of sugar" approach to providing such a component. She went on to say: "We have had a very strong information literacy [IL] program at our library for decades. It is true that professors aren't required to bring their classes to the library, but many choose to do so. I just wanted to make IL more fun for both the students and myself."

The Games

"Goblin Threat"

Arguably, the most popular of her efforts was what she titled "Goblin Threat," created in 2009.

> It is an entirely online game, designed as an alternative avenue for teaching plagiarism education. I knew there was a need for an alternative method of plagiarism education on our campus based on conversations with faculty. The game has been successful on our campus and continues to be assigned by our faculty as part of their courses. What I did not anticipate was how popular it would be with librarians and English instructors at other schools and colleges. After our library's homepage, it is our most-visited site.

She explained that the site had more than 90,000 page visits in 2013 alone. When you consider the fact that the school only has a student population of approximately 1,400, those are fairly remarkable numbers. The numbers seem to come from the assignment of the game to students by other schools in other systems. The game itself was designed in Flash and built from scratch. It is basically a quiz or puzzle-style game, encased in small narratives about freeing various spaces in the school of goblins. You seek the goblins and answer the questions they pose about plagiarism, with increasing difficulty. Broussard states that it was not difficult to create the game, using Flash as a platform and a copy of *Beginner's Flash Game for Dummies* as a guide.

Broussard had also tried other information games geared toward information literacy. One was called "Secret Agents in the Library." With the participation of several professors, it was assigned as part of their introductory English classes. The students found it fun to do the first several semesters it was introduced. The following semesters, as she described it, it did not seem to encourage the enthusiasm as in previous semesters. While it remained an option for professors to include in their classes, it was not further developed, though she has plans to revisit it.

Harry Potter Night

Broussard also came up with the idea to have a library outreach theme night, with various games in the Lycoming College Library. She used the Harry Potter series as a framework for a variety of themed library games, using elements from the books. The fact that Harry Potter enjoyed such a wide popularity is the hook that the library is using to engage their audience. She incorporated elements of LARPing (live-action role play) into the program, such as decorating the library for the event to resemble locations from the books and placing students into "houses" as featured in the series.

Of the elements she describes in the series, I think the most interesting is the choice to place students into houses. As a freshman outreach activity, it is probably well received by the students as they engage with their fellow students to create relationships.

Broussard started the program in 2006, and over the past eight years the program has added elements to make it more popular and reacted to suggestions from the students who attended the events. This Harry Potter program is a series of games rather than an ongoing gamification system. As new students participate, there is a "set completion" to the games. It is gamified in the sense that it responds to the needs and input of the audience. Broussard commented on educational games and this need to respond: "It is important to take your local culture and the specific constraints of the game into consideration. Educational games must be *adapted* rather than *adopted*." Broussard goes into much more detail about this activity in an article in the spring 2013 *Library Trends*.[1]

NEW YORK PUBLIC LIBRARY

A question that is asked about educational games is whether they can exist in the context of public libraries. Academic libraries have very different populations, relatively homogeneous compared to those of public libraries and generally smaller, and realistically a baseline for needs and knowledge their players are bringing into the experience. Academic libraries can have more refined objectives of what the games need to achieve to be considered a success.

In the public library there is a wide range of demographics to design for and more ambiguous goals. In May 2011, New York Public Library (NYPL) ran "Find the Future: The Game" to increase awareness of its resources and history. It was a giant, two-day scavenger hunt, marking the centennial of the library's Stephen A. Schwarzman Building. It was described in the New Yorker thus:

> The game operated on several levels (anyone can now play a basic version by registering online). A hundred items in the library were marked as "artifacts" by QR tags (those weird square barcodes that smart phones can identify). Around seventy squads made up of seven members each scattered themselves around the library, using iPhones to find and scan the artifacts which would then "mathemagically" unlock a secret power. The powers, in turn, unlocked chapters of the epic book that the five hundred of us would collectively write by 5 A.M. Each chapter held specific assignments that correlated to artifacts unlocked by the squad.[2]

As a game objective, the game itself seems to be purely promotional. It was covered extensively in the press. The game did involve five hundred participants, but was basically promoting a very small part of the collection. However, how it was played was designed to create social engagement with the library as means of self-empowerment. The players were able to have Jane McGonigal, the author of *Reality Is Broken*, oversee the design points; this was an attempt at a serious game. She described the purpose as:

> The game is designed to empower young people to find their own futures by bringing them face-to-face with the writings and objects of people who made an extraordinary difference. Like every game I make, it has one goal: to turn players into superempowered, hopeful individuals with real skills and ideas to help them change the world.[3]

The Game

The game structure was a two-day scavenger hunt in which participants searched for works identified by the library as being written by world-changing authors. There were five hundred physical participants, but the city residents could download an app specially designed to search the library catalog and increase their ability to play in the forty-eight-hour period. It ended with five hundred participants locked in the library overnight and writing about the one hundred items found in the scavenger hunt. What they wrote was bound and placed in the NYPL permanent collection for "as long as the library stands."

Summation

I do not necessarily think that quantitative measurements can define how "good" or "worthwhile" a game is. If we look at the players, the number of authors of the finished product in the form of the book was listed as five hundred. If you consider that NYPL listed 1,955,268 total[4] cardholding members, even with one hundred times as many players as those who physically played by being locked in overnight and contributed as authors, you are looking at 2 percent of the community of *cardholders* engaged in the game. Promotionally speaking, it was well received and widely reported on, so it was perhaps successful in that sense. The participants who blogged on or talked about their experience seemed to enjoy it, so perhaps they were, in McGonigal's word, "superempowered" and created an interesting artifact for the library to house. However, if we consider how we define success, I think the argument could be made that as a game design, it didn't achieve the goals of engagement that most systems would find acceptable for the effort involved with its limited number of participants.

The relatively small success of "Find the Future" doesn't point out that gamification doesn't work, however. I think it does point out that it is hard to create a "game" that appeals to multiple types of players. A gamified system could have elements of play similar to NYPL's game, but as a small part of a larger gamified effort. Let us look at gamification efforts inside libraries.

LEMONTREE/LIBRARYGAME

The most currently recognized gamification attempt for a library is Librarygame. There should be more information on the success of Librarygame by the release of this book. As of this writing, they are still in an "extended beta" as they grow the game in scope and look at the data it returns. This still will prove a useful case study because it is the first attempt of a premade platform for gamification specifically designed for libraries. And although it has not achieved a "final form," the development of the software has important lessons to impart about reacting to an audience or player.

Originally the creation of software company Running in the Halls, Librarygame was only in use in the UK and publicly servicing three universities: University of Glasgow, University of Manchester, and University of Huddersfield. Each was using a variation of the Lemontree version of the game, which they developed specifically for academic libraries. At one point they had advertised a "flavor" called Orangetree on their site; however, as of this writing the Librarygame site is no longer mentioning Orangetree. It may no longer be in active development.

The Concept

The premise was fairly simple.

> Registering to use Librarygame requires a one-time Librarygame > LMS (ILS) account authentication. This establishes a link between the Librarygame user and their actual library account. From this point onwards; when a Librarygame user borrows or returns an item (and other types of activities) the LMS sends this information automatically to Librarygame, where it is processed. Certain activities will earn users points and occasionally award them achievements and badges.[5]

The original idea was to award points for the checkout of books. Library patrons could level up, and there were also points and leaderboards assigned to various categories of books checked out in academic disciplines. Patrons could earn the book badge, which was displayed on the library's site as a heat map, turning from green to red depending on the number of points they had earned.

The Problem

The academic version of Librarygame has been around for more than three years; the University of Huddersfield adopted it in 2011. What they had noticed was a correlation between the people who used the library electronic resources and those who achieved academically, which did not correlate to actual visits to the library. The conclusion that Huddersfield made was that people who used the library's physical space were doing so for a lot of nonacademic or noncheckout purposes. To encourage people to use the actual physical collection, Librarygame's first design iteration was to reward checkout.

The idea of a book heat map was ideal for this specific objective: physically checking out books. How successful it was at actually encouraging this behavior is still being reviewed. There has been no declaration of success, but they have continued to develop it at Huddersfield.

Growth

The results must have been interesting enough to attract the interest of the University of Glasgow and University of Manchester. Compared to Huddersfield, Glasgow and Manchester, according to their presentation at ELAG2014, "Librarygame—Evaluating Gamification as a Means of Increasing Customer Engagement," focused more on using

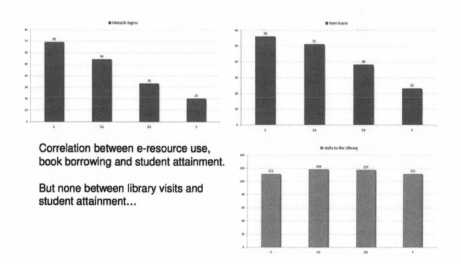

Figure 4.1.   Andrew Walsh, "Gamifying the University Library," Online Information Conference, November 29–December 1, 2011, London.

the physical parts of the library and expanding the socializing aspects of the game than Huddlesfield's focus on book use.

They have run beta tests, and by November 2014, they had been able to display some results. They had introduced the freshmen and upper classmen to revamped versions of Lemontree, with stronger social linkage and social sharing. They reported that the freshmen found it very useful while the upperclassmen had not found it as useful. However, the part of the game the upperclassmen did find interesting was the ability to share book reviews and ratings. While the freshman enjoyed the badges and points for library checkout, what seemed important to the students tested were the social aspects. Some of this effort has been reflected on the Librarygame website as "a fresh social discovery interface" for your library. The communication between students concerning their library use seems to have been beefed up in Librarygame's recent past.

The other major change that came out of Glasgow's and Manchester's involvement seems to be that the Librarygame has switched from being a "one size fits all application" to bespoke software. It is customized to the individual organizations that buy into it. This is reflected in the fact that Glasgow and Manchester had different branding for the game at their two universities: Librarytree and BookIn. They customized it as needed to their player audience. They launched it farther in the 2014–2015 academic year and hope to have more feedback from this effort.

Conclusion

While these universities are thorough with their research, I think we can draw some assumptions from the way the game has been developing if not the preliminary studies. The fact that it has been rebranded and focuses on increasing the social engagement aspect of the design is the area we most want to emulate. The fact that their upperclassmen were not as engaged by the points and leaderboards could likely be because the act of checking out books and digital resources was a skill they already possessed. The fact the freshmen enjoyed this may suggest that the act was more interesting to them from a novelty perspective if nothing else. It is possible that the upperclassmen were simply not challenged by the game. If you consider the idea of flow, it's easy to understand there would be little challenge for players who have knowledge of checkout and do it regularly, so it is not an obstacle to overcome; rather, the points would be easily gained. However, the fact that they did enjoy the new social aspects is encouraging for gamification efforts in public and other libraries.

We can see that the positive aspects of the social sharing of books through libraries can be more easily emulated. The idea of blogging the week's most requested books and allowing reviews and suggestions of books by users who have read it is within most systems' abilities. We will need to see how the data plays out, but it is possible that the element of sharing could increase the engagement by the student body. If it does, libraries may not need to wait to incorporate social elements of gamification until Librarygame is widely and cheaply available.

The other aspect that is worth paying attention to is the fact that Librarygame has continued to develop. As librarian Carian Tabot, who was working on the joint Manchester-Glasgow version, said in his presentation, "The project is about gamification and playing; let's play with our data." So they are going to continue to explore how gamification is affecting the basic processes and the possible outcomes, not drawing assumptions but looking to see how it is used. This is again one of the basic tenants of gamification: changing over time and reacting to users' feedback to optimize systems.

ANN ARBOR—"THE SUMMER GAME"

For a more mature and, in my opinion, better example of a library gamification effort, we can look at the Ann Arbor District Library (AADL) System. For the past four years, they have been running "The Summer Game." It also looks to drive library engagement through a BPL system, but it takes a fairly different approach from Lemontree/Librarygame, one that seems to be paying off. Eli Neiburger, the assistant director, told me that they have seen program attendance triple since running the game.

The Problem

Neiburger told me that the premise was based on feedback from the "classic summer reading program." It used the same format that most public libraries use for the incentive and goal: read ten books over the summer and win a prize.

One observation was made multiple times by parents: "Summer reading programs make my kids read less." The insight was that by limiting the library list to ten books, the children responded by thinking that reading ten books was "sufficient" for the summer. As Neiburger related it to me, the feeling was that the library, as the authority on reading, gave tacit approval to stop reading at ten books; that their "reading duty" was done. This is, of course, antithetical to how summer reading is supposed to affect kids.

The other more interesting piece of feedback heard was from the participants. The YA readers were upset and felt it was unfair that someone who, as Neiburger related it to me, "read *Captain Underpants* ten times" would get the same reward as a participant who pushed themselves to read ten challenging books over the summer. While Neiburger did not necessarily agree that there was a problem with the summer reading program meeting its objective if that happened, he did understand that as "players," the needs of that subset needed to be addressed.

The Game

AADL responded by creating a game on top of their summer reading program, so that the library summer reading program could be incorporated into the larger gamification of the library service. In essence, patrons could "win" a badge and points for summer reading. They offered more badges than just one for each book. Eventually, they ended up with a format where different badges were released throughout the summer that could be gained; the creation and choice of the badges was not preset but was developed in response to the players and gameplay. Summer reading was a gateway for the other badges awarded in categories created by librarians on various subjects and for certain activities including programs and, at one phase, visiting local historic locations.

In "The Summer Game" proper, points are awarded for the different activities, including reading, discovering codes in different areas of the library, attending programs, and participating in different rotating activities. The points can then be redeemed for prizes not unlike arcade tickets, all with the library brand. In my opinion, the important part is that they did not limit what could be of value to the game. In Neiburger's words, "The first thing we needed to do was make it fun." As it developed, the activities changed and were driven by the players' interests.

The original introduction of badges for the categories of reading, viewing, or attending were introduced by the librarians but modified or expanded by the players' feedback. Other elements were introduced wholly from the ideas of the players; a puzzle badge being an example of a badge introduced by the players.

Range of Motion

AADL created a wide range of motion for players to play as they liked. They never specifically used that term in describing their system, but functionally that is what they created. The idea of letting the players push the badging system, creating learning and point-earning opportunities in a wide range of activities rather than focusing on a single objective like reading, has much to do with its success. No small part of this is Neiburger's philosophy behind the gamification system and libraries. He said, "We wanted it to be a game first, be fun first. . . . We took reading out of the name because we wanted it to be about more than just books. . . . We libraries have pigeonholed ourselves, being all about books." By not focusing on what some feel is problematic with the "brand" of the library, and focusing instead on learning and engaging the players on their own terms, and by trying to make the game fun, AADL hit the major parts of gamification. In my opinion, they also made a real connection with the primary purpose of libraries, which is learning, in whatever context or medium is available.

The Response

The payback of this effort by AADL is quite impressive. A YA summer reading program has grown to an all-inclusive program played by whole families. The video on AADL's site for "The Summer Game" features families who are playing the game together, and Neiburger stated that he has more adult players than children now. So the games have a uniting rather than isolating effect on the families that play. I mentioned the program attendance has tripled, but more interestingly, they have created a sense of community among their players. Julie Judkins, a digital librarian for the University of Michigan, wrote in her blog:

> An unexpected benefit of the Summer Game was the strengthened sense of community among players. Although players mostly completed tasks in AADL's Summer Game alone, a strong sense of camaraderie emerged in the comment sections every time a new set of badges was "dropped" and players began to work through the challenges.[6]

Neiburger stated that blog posts have dramatically risen on the site. Players share hints with each other on the library blog, even going to the extent of encrypting their hints so that they don't ruin it for others.

The Technology

There is a downside to this story. "The Summer Game" relies on a decent amount of custom coding. Their development team is creating and running their site in the Drupal CMS. It is not an effort that could be undertaken by every library by any means; however, Neiburger pointed out that the Mozilla Open Badge framework could work as well. If you are interested, AADL does offer their code as an open-source Drupal plug-in for you to use. Many of the projects in this book could be incorporated into a larger effort such as this. You can access and download their plug-in on their GitHub account here: https://github.com/aadl.

CONCLUSION

I think we can see that serious games and gamification have some commonality, and both look to achieve certain similar goals. The question is how do they relate to each other. I think gamification is the larger context in which serious games can sit. When you have a wide audience, it may have to be acceptable to have small return for individual aspects of a larger gamification element. Neiburger stated, "Gamification as a word involves deception. 'The Summer Game' playing is its own reward." I think this is true; the games do need to be fun. The serous game elements show the dynamics of the game; how you win the points is both the source of pleasure and the lesson.

NOTES

1. M. Broussard, "No Muggles in the Library Tonight! Harry Potter Night at an Academic Library," *Library Trends* 61, no. 4 (2013): 814–24.

2. E. Lerner, "Game Night at the N.Y.P.L." *The New Yorker*, May 23, 2011.

3. "Jane McGonigal and NYPL Present Find the Future: The Game," http://www.nypl.org/blog/2011/04/01/jane-mcgonigal-and-nypl-present-find-future-game (retrieved December 21, 2014).

4. "Systemwide Statistics: Fiscal Year 2000," http://www.nypl.org/system-wide-statistics-fiscal-year-2000 (retrieved December 21, 2014).

5. Sam Croft, http://samcroft.co.uk/2012/running-in-the-halls-launches-li-brarygame/ (retrieved December 16, 2014).

6. J. Judkins, "Ann Arbor District Library Summer Game: Building Community," https://thatklickitat.wordpress.com/2012/10/19/ann-arbor-district-li-brary-summer-game-building-community/#more-1681 (retrieved September 30, 2014).

5

STEP-BY-STEP LIBRARY PROJECTS FOR GAMIFICATION

GAME DESIGN: WHERE TO BEGIN

If you're ready to take the first step toward project development, the following games will get you started. I am going to give you several universal examples that might help you create your vision for your game. However, gaming has no limits; if there are parts of the game that your players don't seem to like, you can change it. If you try to make a game and it doesn't turn out as well as hoped, you can change it. If you think you have a better way to make a game than the suggestions I give you, then try it your way. It's all about your library and your players' needs.

HOW TO GAMIFY STAFF ORIENTATION

The first game is for the library staff to play and is focused on staff development. It is best for new employees or volunteers, and it encourages good customer relations. Some of the tools are ones you may be familiar with; they are simple to use and there are only some basic instructions. This project will illustrate how a game can make people think differently: how the mechanics of the game will teach a lesson, not just the "win" conditions.

Through the dynamics of gameplay, one can encourage multiple objectives. The following game would be best for small groups of people as an introduction to the library. While one person can play, a small group of three or more will create an element of competition. It can be modified for different areas the staff may have access to and modified for different departments or sections of a library.

Game: Badge Hunt

Objective: Find all areas of the library and meet the staff there.

Reward: Badges, professional development

Gamification Objective: Increases awareness of other staff as well as physical areas and resources in the library.

Mechanics:

1. Create a map of the library, designating badges that represent each section you want the player to visit.
2. Set the rules based on the number of players.
3. Give the players the map and a time limit to follow it.
4. Send players out to fill in the slots available for the various badges with the names of the people in the assigned sections.
5. Compare the areas players have discovered.
6. After completing the above task, give the players a flow chart with one or more processes representing a major activity within the library, such as how a book goes into circulation.
7. Ask the players to identify the people they met in each section and where each is located on the map. If you have more than one player, reward the person who has the most names of the staff and their job titles.

Alternatives:

This game can also be used for a staff day activity to introduce staff to other members of the library, helping them to understand their duties in relationship to the other departments. The game can also be played with just a map of the collection to introduce people to the physical layout of the library.

1. Create a Map of the Library

This can be a daunting task if we don't know where to get a map. You may know the layout of the library in your head, but drawing one is harder than it sounds, especially if you're trying to keep it true to scale. A secret of mine about where to find a map in the library is to try the emergency exit signs; maps are often there if nowhere else. If you have Photoshop or another image manipulation program, you can snap the image and isolate the layout. There are several online photo-manipulation tools as well. If any of that seems daunting, you can always download and print the map and trace relevant spaces to be found.

If creating a map of public spaces only, black out or remove staff access areas.

2. Design the Badges

1. The next step is to make a badge representing the various areas of the library. In the tools and applications chapter, we covered badge generators. You may choose one from there, create a badge with Microsoft Word, download a free icon set, or just use clip art that you like.
2. You'll want to find an appropriate badge for each department or section of the library that your players will visit. While badge makers are useful, sometimes it is hard to find one that will make a badge specific enough for your use.
3. Place your badges on the map where they correspond to staff or sections to be found. If possible, print the map in color; color makes maps more fun.

3. Identify the Players

The number of players is very important to how this game is played. If you're only doing one or two players, it is important to make sure that the players visit all the departments. For them, *earning* every badge, by visiting every department, is necessary since there will be no one to share or compete against. You will want to make sure that they know where each department is. This is the way to set up the game for a small branch or a library, one that doesn't need to orient often.

However, with more players, you do not need to make it mandatory to visit every department. For this alternative, a variation of the setup of the map is to keep areas blank, and have the staff in each section hand out badges to the players as they visit. This way of setting up your rewards would be more in keeping with gamification as players earn a badge instead of already having them placed on the maps. They get the sense they are exploring and discovering. This way of earning a badge is more competitive, and each badge is feedback for successfully discovering a department. How many badges they can find and finding different ones from other players will make the game more exciting. It will allow some people to get badges others weren't able to get. It may be worth the investment to consider stickers as a way to hand out badges. Then the player can place them on the map as something physical to show the other players.

Another fun idea is to drop a "secret" badge somewhere in the library, such as in the stacks. Place a badge on a table with an "if you find me, take me" note. It is an instant Easter egg since there is no staff there to actually hand it out, and the players will be looking for staff.

Setting Parameters

I would suggest setting a time limit to the game. A time limit could be a mechanic of the game to help see who can get the most badges. When the time is up, have them return to a location. Let the players share the badges they found and if they found different badges. Then have them share what they learned about those departments. Gamification is all about adjusting the game to how your players play so they can get the most out of the experience and you can get the best results.

4. Give the Map to Your Players and Explain the Rules

> Directions: Walk around the library exploring each section. Find a person who has a badge for that section and find out their name, what they do, and something about them. Repeat as needed, and return inside the time limit.

You can give them a sheet to fill out, either before they leave or when they return. If there is only one person in a section of the library, only give it one slot for a badge. If there are twenty, give them four or five. Remember, the goal is to get them to be introduced and interact with as many staff as possible. You may place the questions to be asked on the map, or you can put it on another page with badges next to blank spaces to write the answers to the questions to be asked.

5. Exploring the Library and Meeting Coworkers

A good guide for the time limit is ten to fifteen minutes per section. A new employee or a volunteer will take weeks to interact in a meaningful way and talk to employees outside of their direct job duties. The more time they have, the better to meet other people and talk with them. Your staff will be thankful for this the first time they need to ask the new person to get something and they don't have to explain how and where to send a new person in the library. Also, it gives the rest of your staff a chance to meet the players and a ready topic of conversation to break the ice at that first meeting (even if that topic is how silly it is to *have* to play a game on your first day).

From a human resources viewpoint, this activity also allows the players to interact with other departments, allowing them to not only feel a little more comfortable going there, but also giving them a better idea of who the actual people are that make the library run through personal interactions.

6. Processing the Game with the Players

When the players return, ask them to compare whom they have met. Reward the player who has the most names. Discuss the duties of some of the people met.

Next it is time to give players a new chart, a flow chart describing common library processes. Think of what it takes for something like getting a book into a patron's hand. First there is purchasing a book, then getting it cataloged and shelved, and then checked out. There can be other steps for this or a completely different process, but make a flow chart for the process or processes you decide on.

If you need help creating a flow chart, there are several ways to do this. Downloadable software, online software, or even making one in Word are all option for creating flow charts. I made one in Word using the shapes options on the "Insert" tab. Word also has SmartArt, which includes some premade graphics that could be used. You don't need more than circles and arrows to draw the process. Have the player list the department and names of people responsible for these duties.

7. Ask Players to Fill Out the Sheet; Let Them Compare Notes

Let the players know that the person with the most answers will be the winner. The social aspect of this game is inherent; by adding this competitive aspect, it will appeal to more people, especially that new employee looking to make a good impression. To some degree this competition will appeal to all four "player types." The explorer and achiever will feel a reward in reaching the most areas, while the socializer and the killer will be satisfied by simply gathering the most data. Players who don't win still walk away with a better sense of their place in the organization.

Alternatives

The way this game is structured leaves it open to various applications. Give each member of the staff a badge for their department and keep a list of the badges for a staff day. In a larger organization where individuals rarely interact, this game can be useful for people to get to know each other. If you use the process chart in this situation, it can give them a better idea of their position in the organization. You can also use more than one process, giving individuals different ways to find the information they need and rewarding the person who talks to the most staff in the library. Still another option is to use the map as a tool to identify various parts of the collection. Or just use that map with icons for subjects, reference, or media. Hand it out to new volunteers or patrons to orient them to the physical layout of the building. Reward them for finding a title or resource from each area. Even if they were not interested in playing, it would make a good guide to the physical layout of the library and what resources are available.

HOW TO GAMIFY PATRON SERVICES

Do you have patrons who use Facebook? Many patrons use social media all the time, and getting those patrons to participate on Facebook can be an easy platform for both competition and engagement. People question the effectiveness of using social media, but a better question is how to use it effectively. A good way to use it effectively is to help you recognize employees and promote services with some simple social networking apps.

The game would seem, on the surface, very similar to those in sales competitions because it creates a leaderboard displaying who has been rated highest for their service. While similar, it has important differences. A sales leaderboard is strictly competitive. It offers only one kind of reward—monetary. And it appeals to only one kind of player—the "killer" type. While the game is competitive, it also relies on the social aspect of our jobs. Public employees probably have at least one fan or patron who likes them, and we can capitalize on those established relationships and give employees recognition for fostering them.

Patron recognition is a reward in itself, but they can also compete against others in their departments or library and leave tips for other players. The combination of a reward and giving them a platform to compare their ratings with others is not only satisfying for the staff member, but can hopefully raise awareness of the necessity of good customer service. This type of game illustrates who is liked and lets staff see comments about why they were liked.

This can also serve as a tool for management to see who is popular with patrons. All too often an employee's performance is only known by the complaints they receive rather than positive comments. This game is a way to evaluate and develop professional relationships between staff and patrons. It can allow patrons an opportunity to express both likes and dislikes, not only about staff but about your library services or resources. Of course, this can be moderated to remove offensive, unhelpful, or hostile comments from public and staff view. However, for the manager, it is a venue to receive complaints and have a better idea of what interactions are transpiring.

Another benefit is the game mechanics themselves. When someone uses Facebook to like your content, either from a web page, a blog, or on Facebook itself, they share that information among their peers. This information not only appears on your page, but also the pages of the people who like or share the page. Comments and descriptions of what patrons like about the library or the services of your staff also draw attention to the services the library offers. It will raise awareness of how popular a staff person and the library are within your community and among people who underutilize your library services. The people who truly appreciate us may not share that socially, but by asking them to help an employee, we are getting them to promote the institution, while also encouraging employees to improve their customer service skills.

Game: Face of the Library

Objective: Recognize staff that achieves outstanding customer service.

Reward: Karma, social status, bonuses

Gamification Objective: Incentivize public services staff and evaluate library services.

Mechanics:

1. Set up unique pages for staff, preferably on a blog.
2. Include social sharing icons.
3. Create a visible way to connect to the page at desks or in public use areas.
4. Encourage sharing and comments from patrons.
5. Monitor the shares or likes and give rewards on a timetable.

Alternatives: A blog-type page or page that allows commenting is preferable. It would of course have to be moderated, but it would also allow negative feedback to track employee interactions. You may also allow for voting and social popularity plug-ins for rating employees at libraries. A voting plug-in gives patrons the chance to "rate" an employee. There are plug-ins that rank posts by social popularity; these will rank blogs by how many times they have been shared (http://socialmetricspro.com/social-popularity-widget-addon/).

1. Create a Web Page for Public Service Librarians (Sorry, Technical Services People)

It could be created on your website or on a special blog. I suggest WordPress. Simply go to https://wordpress.com/ and choose "create website."

- You will to need to create an account by offering an e-mail and creating a user name and password (remember you may want to have multiple staff use this, so choose an easy-to-remember password).
- You will have to name your blog. You will want something generic as your title, like the name of your library and the name of the game.
- Now you need to choose a template. Let me suggest something free like "Visual." It is a square blog entry format that will allow multiple staff to be viewed.
- Create a blog entry for all of your chosen staff. If you look at the blog entry screen, you will see that you can add an image. Add a picture of the staff person, or use avatar generators, if you prefer, and some text about the employee. A small bio should feature how long the staff member has worked there, her or his position, her or his favorite book, or some personal tidbit or quote.

The process for doing this is described in greater detail in the book of this series *WordPress for Libraries* by Chad Haefele.

Tip: When setting up the page, you will of course want to be mindful of your employee's privacy, so use their first names only. Some people are very adamant about not having their picture taken. There can be a variety of reasons, and it may seem like that is not a fight you want to take on. One option is to use one of the avatar generators described in the previous chapter to make a cartoon version of the staff; make it recognizable and include their name and department. Some simple text such as "Betsy at Springfield Library helped me today" can be enough for the purpose of the game, but encourage the staff to put some of their personality into their page. (If you let the staff have some level of personalization, they will also feel more engaged in the game; it may help to give them some sense of ownership over the page.)

2. Track Social Sharing

If you've chosen to use a blog site such as Blogger or WordPress, there will be a way to track social sharing. The page will have a share button and the analytics you need to collect your data. WordPress allows you to see the total number of shares. On Blogger or any other content management system, you will have a social sharing widget. A widget or app like +AddThis is a piece of software that will let you share across multiple platforms like Facebook, Google+, or Pinterest and also keeps track of how many people have shared your page.

If for some reason, either institutional or personal, you prefer not to use an existing platform like WordPress, there is a simple bit of code from Facebook that will create a "like" Facebook icon and a link for liking and sharing on Facebook. The code can be found at https://developers.Facebook.com/docs/plugins/share-button. You would want to choose the parameters *box_count* or *button_count* under the layout settings. Click on the "Get code" button. Applying this code will give you an ongoing count of who likes the page. All social networks will have an API page like this. The advantage of using Facebook is that it auto-generates the code and explains how to use it.

One of your options for embedding the code is an IFrame. Select that and copy and paste the HTML code directly into a web page for each employee's page. I would mention there are other options for HTML5 and JavaScript. IFrames are preferable to be backward compliant for patrons with older browsers; HTML5 is a better choice for use with mobile devices, but older versions of Internet Explorer will not be able to use the code.

3. Make the URL Available to Patrons to Select

You have to make it easy for engagement; as a game for the employees and the patrons, we want to provide the patrons an easy way to vote for their favorite employee. One option is a QR code generator, like https://www.the-qrcode-generator.com/. It is easy to figure out what the URL is from visiting the web page or WordPress page blog; type it in and print one for each employee. Or you can just make one QR code for the blog, with a list of all the employees on it and let the patron choose the employee. The latter would be preferable for a large library or system where the patron may interact with several employees in a visit. That way, when they visit the page to "like" a staff member, they will see all or more of the staff; hopefully they will look for other staff they have interacted with in the past. It will give them an opportunity to "like" them as well.

4. Create the QR or Create a Poster Featuring the Blogs

Show your patrons their opinions count and ask them to vote for their favorite employee at the library by liking on the blog and/or sharing their pages on social media. It is also suggestible to put the URLs on the page, as well for how to download QR readers from either the Android or Apple app stores. The URL will be for people without smartphones. By encouraging them to use the QR code reader, you can introduce it to patrons for future use.

5. Keeping Track of Your Game

Use the "like" button to discover the number of times the blog page has been shared. If you are using a plug-in that can promote the blogs by number of shares, or display them by number of shares, use it. Otherwise, I would suggest making a very simple leaderboard; in this case use the "likes" as points for the number of shares.

You might be surprised to learn that everybody in the library has a fan somewhere. Something else you could do is encourage employees to get comments worth five extra points, positive, negative, or indifferent.

HOW TO CREATE A LEADERBOARD

When you are ready to set up a leaderboard, there are simple or complex ways to do it. You will notice that I used the box_count command from Facebook to allow you to discover the number of "shares." You could use the box count to simply create a list in order of the post/employee with most number of shares. Many of the WordPress plug-ins will allow you to share across more social networks than just Facebook. There are also sharing plug-ins that will allow you to view analytics, or statistics, which include the most shared post. In this case, where a post is dedicated to a single employee, you can easily take that list and then organize it by popularity.

In either case, you need to decide whether the leaderboard will be available to the public, meaning the patrons can see it, or only for the staff to view. I would suggest outward facing. It would encourage patrons to follow the progress of favorite employees. I would also suggest that, though there are ways to arrange posts by number of shares, you don't want to do this. First, it will not include extra points for comments; second, it would immediately make some people seem more popular than others and affect the results. Also avoid putting negative consequences for negative comments or using a voting app where people can vote something *down*. Remember, we are looking for *positive* engagement.

My suggestion is to simply take the raw data and make a simple list of leaders based either on number of shares or number of shares plus the outcome of multiplying the number of positive comments by five. You can of course experiment with how this displays, maybe thumbnail images of the staff next to their name. However, this approach will work easily for any web system you put your "likeable" posts on, whether that is WordPress, your own site, or special Facebook pages.

Decide on a period of time, such as a month, and offer a reward for the leader each week and one for "most improved." When the month is over, give the overall winner a bigger reward.

This game can be more effective than an average customer survey to raise awareness about who visits the library and hopefully provide some useful information on how people interact with staff. Adding the game elements of leaderboards, you may motivate the staff to participate more. Also, by adding the ability to vote and leave comments, it gives patrons a way to feel like they are doing something nice for the staff, while giving you analytics and promoting the library.

Alternatives: A couple of other options for this game are:

- Departments can compete, especially in large system branches.
- You can also put prompts at the bottom of the pages for blog posts, such as "tell us why you like this librarian/library" or "what would you like to see changed/added to the library/blog." Remember, the staff gets five extra points for comments, so let them ask patrons to comment.
- Also let patrons not on social networking know they can "vote" through commenting.

GAMIFY YOUR PROGRAMS BY INCLUDING BADGES

Badges are the first things we think of when we think of gamification. They are the visual representations of achievement that are awarded to players in many online games. We will be using Credly to create, issue, and display these badges. We are using this application in place of Open Badges since it is still in closed beta; however, Credly does integrate with Open Badges. It is very possible that the Mozilla Open Badges Badge Kit will be out of beta by the time this book is published, and you may want to consider using it. The other option is to simply make badges as stickers to hand out.

One of the benefits of badging is that it does not need to be limited to your library and programs. If you run a summer program such as an introduction to computers, perhaps a local organization offers Microsoft Word classes and would be willing to participate and tell the patron a new badge is available to them if they take the class there.

Create a Credly Account

Go to http://credly/com to create an account. Make sure to choose the organization option when you sign up. You may set up your profile as you like, but make sure to link your social media to the account (Facebook, Twitter, LinkedIn, etc.).

Game: Summer Fun around the City

Objective: Attend a different program in each branch or a variety of branches.

Reward: In this case, it is just a more entertaining way of doing what is usually done but with clearer proof of attendance and better promotion.

Mechanics:

1. Find a map of the city and turn it into your passport.
2. Create a badge or logo for each branch and slots on the map.
3. Give the players a map and a time limit.
4. Send them out to fill in one or more slots of the passport for the various branches, with names of programs in that section.
5. The first three people who complete the passport get their picture posted online. Everyone who completes the passport gets a special completion badge or reward.

1. Find a Map

You can use a map of the city and mark your locations or other opportunities to get badges on the map. This should be easy to acquire. If you're stuck, contact the tourist bureau and get a city map. Scan it into your computer.

My library system would have something like figure 5.1 for a map.

Also make several different badges for wild cards. If your library does outreach to farmers' markets or maker fairs, you can take some of the wildcard stickers with you. However, you will want to make a special badge for the specific event so people can compare and share wildcard badges.

2. Create Badges

You will need to make a badge or logo for each branch. For instance, in my city, I have nine branches, so I might require ten stamps, from at least five different branches.

In your Credly account, create a badge for each branch, or several programs at each branch, as well as wild cards. To use the badge generator:

1. Choose a shape.
2. Create a logo inside of the shape.

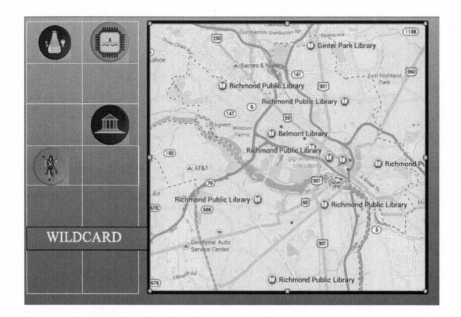

Figure 5.1. Map data ©2014 Google.

3. Add a banner with some text.
4. Name the badge. It will be able to be rewarded to people as they accomplish the different objectives.
5. Download the image and make stickers from it for the players, so their paper passport will reflect their digital ones.
6. When you save this badge, it will take you to Step 2.
7. In Step 2 there is a drop-down menu; choose to give the credit to anyone with the code.
8. Credly will auto-generate a code; write this down to give to patrons when you give them the sticker badges, so they can claim it online. The code can also be given out to community partners to award wild cards.
9. Make sure to print off each of the badges for the programs as stickers to put on the printed map as well.

Add credit description information in the badge box, so people can see how to earn the badges when players share them. It is important if you do outreach programs, so that people know they are available and where you have been.

Figure 5.2.

If you don't do outreach, another option might be to talk to a community partner and advertise that attending their event is worth a special wild card. You can also allow the partner to take an e-mail address or create a claim code in order to get the badge and give the digital badge to the patrons right at that moment. The award will be viewable later on, and the library can check and then give a sticker at the desk the next time the library patron visits. Also, create a few badges that can be "gifted" by players to other players for wild-card slots. A good example is if one of your programs is a book club. You can have a great commenter badge, and allow that to be awarded by patrons.

As the issuer of badges, you can accept an invite to give a badge; let the players know these are available as wild cards. They can submit them to you by sending the other player's e-mail to you and the badge they wish to award. If they have joined Credly, they can make an invite for the other player through their account. Consider letting patrons award a badge to the presenter of programs as well, and then issue them a recognizer badge.

3. Send the Players Out

When they attend a program, they can get their sticker for a program. They also will get the digital badge. Be prepared to help them sign up for Credly. It is not a difficult process. All it requires is a usable e-mail address, and this is also a good place to use the avatar generators. Keep track of your patron's e-mail; remind them when they have badge opportunities. The players will need to fill out their passport in an allotted time.

4. Rewards the Players Who Complete the Passport

The first player to fill in all ten slots will get a prize. In this case it can be a new badge and promotion that they finished the passport game. An option is to have the players choose a "home branch." Award one from each branch as well. So a first-time badge will be available at all the branches. A completed passport gets another badge; anyone with all ten slots and the two wild card slots get an extra badge.

The benefit of this game is twofold. One, you get contact information, and once they are in the game system, you can continue after the passport game to award badges. Two, you can create special badges on the fly and make them more wild-card badges. Make a badge for integrating into Facebook or Twitter, to encourage social sharing. After the actual game is done, you can keep awarding badges for whatever reason, including completing the other projects in this book. If you try to create some of the games, include the code for a completion badge in the final screen of the games.

Again, I would like to stress that this *integrates* with Open Badges, and there is a BadgeOS for WordPress that this also integrates with. If you have a WordPress site or Drupal, you can integrate using BadgeOS instead. Another feature of Credly is that it can integrate with programs like MailChimp, so you can send out reminders. It also lays the groundwork for more integration of badges for ongoing programs beyond summer.

Tip: The claim code is a great option to use in conjunction with the other projects in this book. When the patron completes one of the games or projects, you can display the claim code so they can claim their digital badge on Credly or another system. Remember to brand it and give a description including where the game can be played. In this way, you can start tying the projects together in a larger gamification system.

HOW TO GAMIFY YOUR COLLECTION USING
AUGMENTED REALITY TO LINK IT TO YOUR LIBRARY

Libraries contain a little bit of information about everything. One of the reasons that people have questioned our usefulness in modern times is that it seems to be constrained by our brick and mortar institutions. The information about objects, events, and history of our community seems constrained by the fact that going to the library is a special trip. We know why someone uses our online public access catalog (OPAC): to find information. It is the how that is the problem. Most people do not know to go to the catalog unless they come in looking for a book, or go to our website in the first place. There is a disconnect between their moment of need and the return of results. Between that moment of need and the results from an OPAC, there are at least five steps:

1. Identify need.
2. Go to library/web page.
3. Search for results connected to need.
4. Find useful results.
5. Obtain materials.

We can decrease that number of steps to the minimum. The game I propose does exactly that and has other benefits as well, like the social sharing and community engagement. Rather than explain it, let me use a tool from UX (user experience, an IT concept), a user story. Think of what those five steps would normally take and compare it to this:

> A community member takes a trip to a fabric store. In the corner of the store is a small image based on your library and some text that says, "Learn how to do more," and a link to the Aurasma app. They have that app, or if they don't they're prompted to download it. They point it at the store and they're launched into a video on their phone: "I'm Betsy/Bill your undercover librarian and you've found Springfield Library's clandestine catalog. We love people who sew; we have many resources and meetings for the fashion designer in you. Double tap to learn more. The patron does and they're brought to a web page with a list of books available at the library on the topic of sewing and a list of upcoming events on fashion. If the library has downloadable eBooks available, a list of eBooks they can download on the spot is also provided, relevant to the location they are in.

Is this a game? It is in the sense that it is a playful way to interact with your community. It is similar to geo-caching or other puzzle games. I talked about the four player types, and this is definitely for the explorer. And although they are not competing in the scenario I described, you can add gaming elements later. You can create competition and social sharing once you have laid the groundwork.

Augmented Reality and a Catalog Easter Egg Hunt

Augmented reality is the term used to describe adding video, graphics, or text to existing images or places that can only be viewed with a device, like an iPhone, iPad, Android devices, or now Google glasses. Augmented reality applications are designed to view an existing object, like a statue or building, and overlay text or animation over it. However, the uses of augmented reality can be scaled down to most libraries' budgets for production and technical capabilities. It is more interesting and easier to add video to a hosted augmented reality app than place a QR code. Not only is it more original, but you can also use real-world physical objects to call up web pages that link to other pages and more information.

Game: Citywide Clandestine Catalog

Objective: Raise awareness in the community about library resources, while also making connections with patrons outside the library.

Reward: A sense of discovery, badges

Mechanics:

1. Set up an Aurasma account.
2. Identify locations where you can create meaningful linkage to your catalog.
3. Create trigger images and signage for placement at chosen locations.
4. Create overlays of video for locations.
5. Make auras and link them to the library's web page.
6. Encourage sharing and comments from patrons on the library's website.

Alternatives: Add an element of competition to the apps such as "Be the first to discover 20 Clandestine Catalog locations," and so on.

1. Create an Aurasma Account

Aurasma is one of the leading players in augmented reality. There are several other competitors in the field. LAYAR is one, but it seems prohibitively expensive. DAQRI.com is a newer one, and DAQRI offers an educator package for free. However, Aurasma is more established and has a selection of channels to call attention to multiple sites. It will notify your device if you are close to an Aura. An Aura is any site or object that has a virtual layer on it from the Aurasma app. It makes discovering new sites easy for the user. Aurasma also charges nothing for the app or creations of sites. Once the user downloads the app and follows the library's selected channel, they will have access to the entire library's content of Auras.

To set up your account simply:

- Go to the Aurasma site: http://www.aurasma.com/.
- Click on the Customers menu item.
- Sign up for an account and it will take you to Aurasma Studio.

The app has a simple tutorial you can follow. First, set up a channel; you should name the channel after your game. It would be wise to also include the name of the library. For this example, name it "Springfield Library's Clandestine Catalog." The website will also offer you a chance to upload an image to apply to the channel; some variation of your library's logo would be best. Be sure to pay attention to the aspect ratio of the image. The image does not need to be "high resolution"; however, it does need to be the right length to width. Aurasma suggests that you use 360 by 240 at 72 dpi.

After the channel is set up, there is a generated URL or web link. It is a static URL so people can subscribe to the library's channel. It can be used on promotional material. Click on the link to subscribe and copy the URL from the pop-up that it generates. The link to subscribe is always located in the channel box in the lower left-hand corner. It can be returned to at any time, so it is useful to know where to find it.

Next, once the channel is established, there will need to be triggers and overlays created. Triggers are images to start "Auras." An Aura happens when an image goes into augmented reality. Overlays are elements of an Aura, which include animation, video, and even text. How-

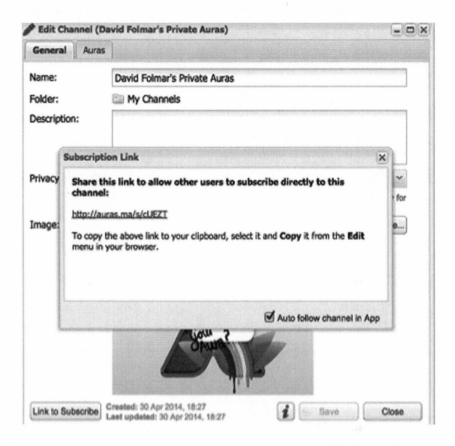

Figure 5.3.

ever, before an overlay and trigger can be created, you'll want to decide what to augment in reality.

2. Select Your Auras

The step of identifying where to place Auras seems simple. Theoretically, a library should have some information on everything. However, you want something thematic or to prioritize what information you refer to. Targeting the information makes it a better game. If you were to use my library, for example, in Richmond, Virginia, a city with considerable history, you would want to identify the historic landmarks of the city and choose them as locations in which to place your Auras. You can always add other locations later. Perhaps your city does not have enough historic areas for Auras to generate a playable game. This game can be used to attract certain demographics such as tweens and teens, so you would focus your Auras on areas and activities that appeal to them.

Another option for the Auras is partnering with local businesses. They might be interested in being site selections since, once someone subscribes to the library's channel, they will show up on your players' devices when they pass or find another Aura in the area. The combination of local libraries supporting local business is a good one, if for no other reason than locally owned businesses have fewer policies about promoting community services. For instance, a local health food store or grocery chain could be a good location. Make a Clandestine Catalog entry for healthy eating, gluten-free cookbooks, or other topics, which will link to the local business in which you have placed an Aura.

3. Create Trigger Images

A trigger image is an image that you point your phone at that will activate an Aura when in a specific location. You need two pieces to create an Aura—a trigger image and to be a particular place. A trigger image could be anything, but I would suggest signs that you place in locations. You need to let people know how to sign up for the game anyway, so why not kill two birds with one stone? If you create signs to use as trigger images, you can also create variations of theme. You can use one trigger image or several; it will depend on the number of locations you create. I would suggest making several signs for different categories: "Springfield Clandestine Catalog: Crafts," "Springfield Clandestine Catalog: History," "Springfield Clandestine Catalog: Food," and so forth. Chose areas of your collection or programs you want to promote for categories.

It is possible to use a building or landmark itself as a trigger. One trigger image could be a historical landmark; one could be of a local business. Once your patrons are using Aurasma, their phones will notify them if they are near an Aura. However, it would not tell them if they had not already downloaded Aurasuma. A sign can do both.

The Aurasma guide will tell you all you need to know about making good trigger images. If you create signs, you can load up a digital version of the sign as a JPEG or PNG file. When creating a trigger image, remember that whether it is a sign or a landmark, pay careful attention to creating or finding contrast in the image. If using a landmark, you'll want to try choosing a time when the image is well lit since image recognition software responds best under well-lit conditions, and a trigger image that works well during the day may not work so well at night.

When you start to load the copies of your trigger image on the Aurasma website, it will ask for a name of the Aura and allow to you to choose a spot on a Google Map where that Aura is created.

Ready to load your first image?

- Go to Aurusuma.com and sign into your account.
- Next go the Aurasuma Studio and select trigger images from the top right.
- Select Add.
- When Add appears, choose a trigger image.
- Name the trigger: "Clandestine Catalog: History," for example, if using historical landmarks or locations.
- Aurasuma will automatically "train" your image for you. This means it will look for contrast and the most important detail and mask out unimportant information. If you use signs and follow the instruction for making a good image, this should not be a problem.
- Click View Maps on the Aurasuma home page; the map will be the whole globe.
- Scroll down to a location on the map and right-click your location and name it. Press Enter.
- You will be asked to write a description. Whether you write a description or not is optional, the location name should actually be enough. However, a description will make it easier for someone else to work on this project.

4. Add Augmented Reality Layers

Now you're going to create the overlays for your images. They will link to a static URL or web page. However, you want something fun to happen. Now keep in mind the app is showing a picture of the trigger image when the overlay starts; it could be as disjointed or smooth as you

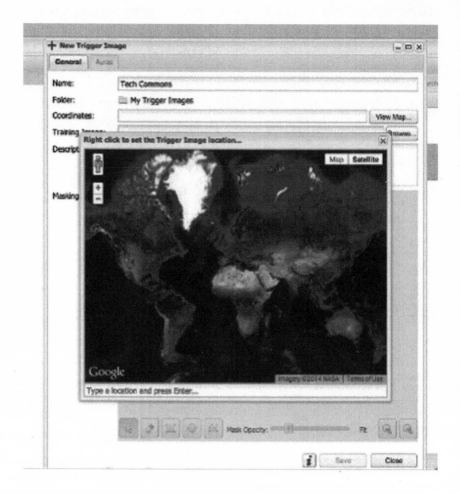

Figure 5.4.

like. It can simply be a new piece of text fading in or as complex as 3D animation. My suggestion is to do a simple video. Find someone with a flair for the theatrical; make it fun. Production quality is not as big an issue as the fun factor. You can use a phone or iPad to make the video.

Tip: A quick tip from twenty years of production experience: you can add quality quickly and cheaply by focusing on audio first. Use a plug-in microphone versus the one built into your phone. Everyone is used to phone or webcam quality video these days, but the microphone built into consumer-level cameras or tablets is very bad at picking up audio from more than a few feet. So a cheap USB or plug-in microphone will add a lot, for a small price. Second, use a tripod or sandbag to keep shakiness to a minimum. Surprisingly, sandbags on a table do a very good job.

You can start your video with someone holding the sign and pulling it down from in front of the camera. Have the person on camera explain to the patron that they have found a Clandestine Catalog location. Have them tell the player to look for other locations in their community. Then tell them to double-tap the screen to find out more. Again, like trigger images, you can have a single overlay for everything or do several for different categories or one for each individual location. Do not feel like it has to be a video. A video would make it more dynamic, but even a graphic saying, "You found a location, double-click now" can link to the library website.

Warning: The maximum size for videos is 100 MB. That is not a lot when it comes to videos, so keep them short. You may have to compress your video files. That sounds scarier than it is; you can recompress video using YouTube. Or download a free compressor here: http://www. freevideocompressor.com/. This is a nice tool to help you compress video and will let you specify the file size you want. There are many other programs out there, but whichever one you choose, simply select export for web and choose a compatible video format such as MP4 or FLV. You will find these options listed on almost every program that compresses video.

Once you're satisfied with the video you've made, add it to your page by going back to Aurasma Studio.

- Click on Overlay; it is on the right-hand side and looks like two butterflies.
- You will need to name it. I would suggest found location. You could have more than one video if you choose, for different types of locations.
- Select the type of overlay. In this example I am suggesting it is video, which is the default option.
- You can skip the description or use this to categorize the overlay for later users.
- Save and close.

5. Finishing Touches

For the final element of the game, there will have to be a web page or web pages to link to. Remember the instructions to build a web page with WordPress? You can use that process again, or create new pages on your library's website. Each page should have several elements:

- Include a reward for the player for finding the page, not a prize, just a "Congratulations on finding another Clandestine Catalog!" It's important to make the player feel they have achieved something. You can also use a Credly badge code to award a badge.
- Link to elements in your catalog. You can simply put down the titles of some books. Or you can create a link for your OPAC, encouraging patrons to look for more entries. If you go to your OPAC through your web page, look at the top of the browser window; there is an address bar there, and it contains the web address or URL of your catalog. You can include that as a link. If you know some HTML, it is possible to submit a set of criteria for the search and have the box filled with relevant data every time the site is visited.
- Include a way to share they found it on social networks. The Facebook share API from the previous project could be used.
- You could also include lists of events that are relevant to the topic along with their start times. Again for the more advanced user, you can link to the events' web pages as well. Do you have a searchable calendar? If you can, put the results of searches related to the topic of the game entry on the web page.
- Make sure you have a comments box on the page. Encourage visitors to leave a comment to let others know they were there.

6. Create the Aura

Once finished with the page, you're ready to do your last work in Aurasma. You will now create your Aura. Remember to keep your locations and trigger images organized. Go to the studio and add an Aura to your page.

This is the most complex of the screens you come across.

- Choose an Aura from the right side of the menu.

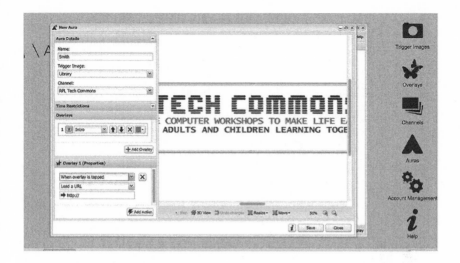

Figure 5.5.

- Choose the Add button in the top right; the window above will then pop up.
- For the Aura to work properly, you need to fill out all the following:

  - On the left is the name. You should name it after the location where the Aura will be.
  - Trigger Image is whatever name you gave the trigger image when it was added. I had suggested "Clandestine Catalog: History" or a specific one like "Empire State Building."
  - For the box marked Channel, use "Springfield Library Clandestine Catalog" or whatever you chose to name your channel.
  - The box named Time Restrictions should only be changed if you planned on ending the game at some point.
  - Overlay would be the video you created. Write in that name "Found Location." If you have more than one video, you would select the appropriate one
  - Next click on "Add Action"; it is recognizable by the lightning bolt on it.

- Choose "when overlay is tapped" or "when overlay is dou-
  ble-tapped" and the action to load URL, and add the URL
  or web address of the pages you created.
- Click Save and close.

You have just used an augmented reality app to place your collection
throughout your city and raise awareness about your library. A complete game would require you to repeat this step for multiple locations.
Some of you might be asking, Where is the game again? The game is in
the discovery of the sites, of knowing the sites are there. It is basically
like geocaching, a puzzle game played in the real world instead of online. In geocaching, players are given GPS co-ordinates to find a secret
item or items and then add something to it for other players. We are
basically creating secret prizes for players to find and comment on, but
instead of a GPS, using an app.

You might like to add a competitive edge to this game. You can do
that by allowing players to post comments. Competitive elements don't
have to be obvious; just enabling comments to be posted on the page is
competitive. It will let the player state when and where they found it.
First, allowing players to add comments is a great way for them to feel
an ownership of the game; it can also be competitive. People who like to
play competitively will notice others who are playing and try and find
Auras that others have not. Want to jump start this competitive process? You can do so by simply asking above the comments "Who found
this first?" Moderate the comments; explain that each player only gets
one comment per page.

If you have the ability, you can keep track of commenters. You could
also add an element that keeps track of frequent or top commenters,
like this WordPress plug-in: https://wordpress.org/plugins/top-
commentators-widget/faq/; you have a de facto leaderboard. The plug-
in shows the top commenters on your page. The plug-in will also allow
you to change the title to whatever you want; it could be called Clandestine Catalog Leaders or something similar. You will have a way to see
who finds the most sites and encourage both comments for social play
and competitive play.

HOW TO GAMIFY INFORMATION LITERACY EDUCATION USING INTERACTIVE FICTION

This next project can be viewed and played on PlayMyLibrary.me. Play through it to have a better idea of how it's put together. You can also start thinking of your own changes to the project to "make it your own." Feel free to comment.

We are going get closer to creating an *actual* video game now. Exciting as that sounds, it is going to be even easier than you think! The reason is that the platform Twine was designed to encourage independent development of games using simple mechanics and graphics to create interactive, non-linear stories. Twine has been around since 2009 and is open source and free to use; it will let you include graphics, logical statements, and JavaScript, all of which you *won't* have to use unless you want to. You can make a very linear story with some simple graphics and a few simple HTML commands that I will give you.

The gamification part of our project is how you tell your story. Players advance through the game by finding certain resources in the library's catalog, which we will embed in the Twine game, using an IFrame. This is an HTML command that lets you place a web page inside another web page. This game will need to be hosted online and have access to your OPAC.

The OPAC resources you want to include can be identified once you have your story line. First, you'll want to find resources from your OPAC using subject search, title search, and at least one author search. In this way you can teach patrons how to use proper search tools, and if so inclined, you can also incorporate advanced searches using Boolean operators in a keyword search, databases you have, or any reliable online resource.

For this game, I chose to do a zombie apocalypse theme. Again you can adjust yours, but other than the huge benefit that the success of zombie themes have from shows like *The Walking Dead*, it has the benefit of showing the real value of a nonfiction collection. When I was doing my collection development class for my MLS, I ran across an article about a contractor converting an old missile silo into "Doomsday Condos." In the diagram was a library. I thought this was an interesting collection problem: a collection not driven by patron usage but by what would be beneficial after society collapsed. All of the information to rebuild society is theoretically in a collection at your library, and that is the premise of this game: not how to destroy zombies, but how to rebuild society afterwards.

Game: Zombies and the Library

Objective: Explain the resources in the library and how to use the OPAC to find them.

Mechanics:

1. Identify aspects of your OPAC and possibly online elements you can use to identify the game objectives your player must overcome.
2. Create an audience-appropriate story for the library.
3. Download Twine and learn some basics.
4. Plot out the story with both positive and negative outcomes.
5. Use Twine to create the story objective including negative consequences.
6. Collect graphics and HTML elements for your story.
7. Output from Twine and find a hosting area.

1. Identify the Aspects of Your OPAC You Would Like to Promote

If patrons don't understand more advanced search functions, OPACs are rarely fully used. Google and other search engines have encouraged a culture of keyword searching. A patron will usually not go any farther than that. Even if they are aware of the OPAC, it's usually used to search by keyword or, in the case of fiction, by author or title. Since our very expensive databases may be underutilized, the goals for better utilization of the OPAC are as follows:

- Call attention to our OPAC.
- Show how to use an OPAC to search by title, author, and subject. Show how subject headings can return a variety of resources.
- Call attention to databases available for use.
- Promote the usefulness of the library's nonfiction collection and the value of it.

Since it is a rather large list of objectives for a game and learning how to use an OPAC is not very engaging, let's nest this in a story. This is a story where the *dynamics* of searching the catalog serves a purpose that appeals to patrons.

2. Create an Audience-Appropriate Story for the Library

When creating your story, always keep your players in mind. When you are creating your narratives, you can think about what you want patrons to learn from your scenario. Keeping the tenets of PERMA in mind, you can encourage them not just to use the ILS, for example, but how to make their lives better. By choosing the right theme, you can encourage them to find out how to do carpentry, masonry, and plumbing, as well as how to look at sources for team building, conflict resolution, and governance. What situation requires those skills? Well, I chose the "zombie" theme because my library, like many, sees a drop-off in patronage after childhood, and the patrons do not usually return until they are parents. Knowing that teens and post–high school readers are already engaged in using the Internet for informational needs, it is an audience the library has to engage and prove value to.

The other factor to consider for your story line is your community. I chose to focus on zombies and the post-apocalypse timeframe. However, I live in a rather conservative area and I might not be able to get away with this; I certainly wouldn't be able to get away with it if I was focused on how to *kill* zombies. I understand that I could find resources in my collection that would teach how to make chainmail or maybe even make weapons. But instead I can focus on more positive aspects of the scenario.

1. I need a story that will appeal to as many people as possible but also not alienate others.
2. We are trying to think of PERMA, positive engagement. Making them think they have the skills to survive a zombie apocalypse is nice. However, having the skills to be self-reliant is a more enabling objective for communities that have to deal with food deserts, economic challenges, and feelings of disempowerment. The idea that they can build their own self-sufficient community has value.

3. What resources am I limiting myself to and how well would my audience be able to relate to its use in their lives? Some effective searches related to rebuilding after the apocalypse might be how to grow food, how to make effective teams, or how to repair plumbing. Can you teach the patrons how to find resources for your objectives in your story?

If you choose to make a different framework, do you have the tools to run a report on your ILS for most popular fiction at your library and identify a theme? Another example might be to do a "Little Library on the Prairie" story line and look for agricultural resources in your nonfiction, as well as animal husbandry and carpentry. There are many aspects of farm living to find using the ILS and Dewey subject headings.

Another story option might be the detective story. For example, your title could be something like "The Long Checkout, Sam Spade in the Stacks" or "Avengers Assemble in the Library." When you know your audience, you can tailor the game to their tastes. Feel free to try several themes; after all, you're a librarian and you have all the inspiration you need around you.

3. Download Twine and Learn Some Basics

The first thing you will do is download Twine. You will need to run this program on your computer. It does not need much in the way of processing power and is currently available for Mac and Windows users (sorry, Linux folks). There are currently downloadable versions of Twine online and a version hosted on GitHub. My suggestion is to go to http://twinery.org/; you will find a page to download the program from there. Be aware there is a beta version being developed; it should have better incorporated responsive elements for tablets and smartphones and supports HTML5. It is not fully functional at the time of this writing, so I am using version 1.4.2.

Once you have installed Twine on your machine, open to the main page. If you are using a Windows operating system, these examples may look a little different from yours, as they are a Mac format.

"Start" is where you begin your story. The three boxes that show up are all important, but the story title and story author are pretty self-explanatory. Once you have filled them in, you need to move on to

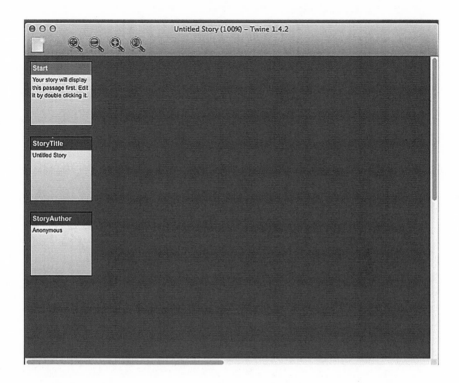

Figure 5.6.

Start. It is important that you do *not* change this box's name. Start tells the program that is the first page that will be displayed.

If you double-click on the icon, it will open. Whatever your story, here is where you grab your players' attention. This is the screen that will display your introduction. You can add images if you like (we will talk about that later), but for now you can use it like a word processor. Simply start typing the opening to your story; it will support the tab function from your keyboard and the return to end a sentence, so you can format the text easily. Beyond that you need to use code; I will supply you with the code you will need for your project.

The bottom part of the story is done in code. Do you see the **[[go there||Library]]**? It is similar to how you link in HTML but easier. Linking the text to the next passage is how you build the interactive part of the Twine game.

- The two [[tell the software that what follows is code.

- **go there** is the text it will display.
- You separate the text with a |. (This can be hard to find; it is above return key and requires you use the shift key.)
- **Library** is the passage you will be taken to.
-]] tells the program you're done putting in code.

When you close the window, a message will pop up asking you if you want to create the new passage you referenced. You can say yes to add it. You have created your first interactive element. Still, it would not be much of a game if the players didn't have options, so we can add an option to not go into the library.

Add a new line, calling up a new passage, for a different option. The line of code would look like this:

> "Too many windows," says Bob. "Let's go someplace [[else !||Zombie Attack]]"
> (Notice the characters inside the brackets are going to be "links," so keep the quotations outside of the closing brackets.)

Adding new options is always the same process, and now there is a second option. In the example above, I named the passages; from the name of the second one "Zombie Attack," you can see me using a little negative reinforcement to get the characters into the library. The goals of the game are to get the player in the library, so there needs to be a negative consequence when they don't go.

When you add in the option using the [[*display words | tile of next Passage*]] format, there will be a prompt to create the new passage option. This is how to make a game, a very short one, but a game nonetheless. To make the game better, the first thing we need to do is create more steps for the completion of the game. We do that by identifying our objectives.

4. Plot Out the Story with Both Positive and Negative Outcomes

The objectives will be to learn the aspects of our OPAC and create searches that would illustrate them. When you have your objectives and your searches, you have the framework of the story to build your game around. You can start to sort out a rough *narrative* to build your *me-*

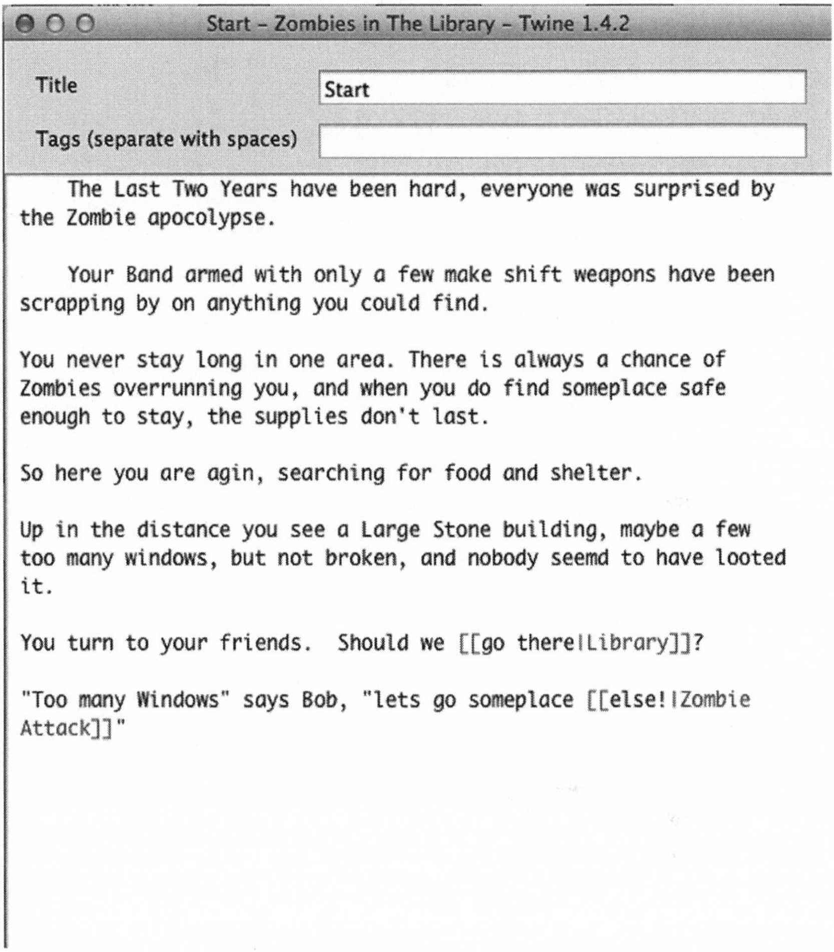

Figure 5.7.

chanics. Remember the game *narrative* needs to be reinforced by game *mechanics*. This is an example of your outline.

I did not sketch out level two and three but just gave you an idea of how to approach them. Now you can use your own resources and game story to make objectives that suit your needs. What I want to bring your attention to is that I did include that there should be increasing levels of difficulty. Rewards are escalated as well. The level structure will give your player an area to get badges that can be shared.

Table 5.1.

Objective	Story Element
Get patrons to library	Get them to take shelter in library and meet their librarian.
Make patrons aware of the value of your collection	The building is insecure from attack; one character wants to burn books to keep warm. Librarian suggests there are better ways to use them.
Call attention to your OPAC	Librarian shows how to use OPAC to look up how to help hurt person.
Search by title	They search OPAC for title *First Aid*.
Search by subject	The library is insecure; they look up "masonry books."
Search by subject	They need food. Search for maps of area for farms or warehouses.
Search by author	The player is having problems keeping the group together. Librarian suggests that Dale Carnegie wrote a book that might help them.
END LEVEL ONE	You are now leader with your faithful librarian friend. However, the situation can not last forever; supplies will run out in time.
USE Boolean Logic OR	
USE Boolean Logic AND	
USE Boolean Logic NOT	
END LEVEL TWO	You are self-sufficient but there is so much more to life than survival. The noble librarian, seeing you capable of using the resources and realizing that you need access to aids to teach the children to read, offers to travel to the state capital where the database is still hosted and get it running again. Or maybe you need to find stores and supplies to make radios.
How to use online databases	
END LEVEL THREE	You use the renewed lines of knowledge to create communication between survivors. You can now reach out and help fellow enclaves. The survivor camps look to you for knowledge and aid.

The game would look like the first option below; to be enjoyable we need to create a challenge, which is why we have the second option.

While you can give immediate negative consequences, you can also give them some freedom of motion, if you choose. Then you can build multiple options from wrong options. You can lead your player back to the original objective, end their game, or add a short third option, so they don't feel like they are being told what to do. You want to give

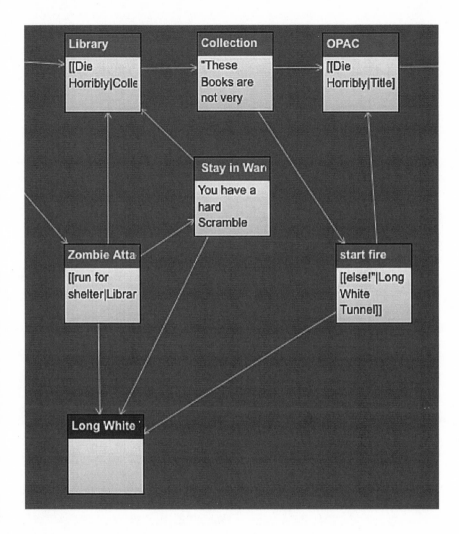

Figure 5.8.

them some range of motion; allow them to go to a warehouse for the night, for example.

5. Use Twine to Create the Story Objectives Including Negative Consequences

You can decide how to make the library an attractive option for your players, but the ability to *not* end the game with the wrong answer is important. If you remember the old choose-your-own-adventure books, they were similar to this. The problem with them, in my opinion, was that you almost always died. You had only one right answer. So the books bored me fairly quickly. You want to keep your players engaged in the game long term, and an ending will end that engagement rather quickly. So building these wrong options that sidetrack an adventure is preferable to just killing them.

It is important to add negative consequences for not getting the correct answers as players progress through the story. Another great feature of Twine is the reuse of passages. When creating a "start fire" passage, instead of creating a new ending, reuse any of the existing ones. By calling them up in the passage part of the format, you let the characters get a little off track before coming back to the objectives of the game. Be sure to take advantage of that.

Now you can provide feedback to your players and make negative consequences that don't end in death. It is also where the fun of the game is for the player. Be as creative as you want. Multiple threads off of one passage, with multiple threads off that passage get confusing fast, especially when you want to reuse something like the zombie attack passage.

Twine allows you to include a passage inside another passage; in code you would call this nesting. You might have something like a "zombie attack" you don't want to repeatedly describe. Here is the trick to that. It is possible to make an unlinked passage from scratch. Using the menu in Twine, there is an option under Story to choose New Passage; or you can use a shortcut (CMND-N on Mac) or simply use the "New Passage" button in the upper right corner.

When you name this passage for repeating, nested in other passages, name it without using any spaces. Machines are not very good at reading blank spaces in file names. So I name this piece of text I want to repeat as "ZombieAttack." Then you display the text inside the other passage using <<display ZombieAttack>>, or you can use just <<ZombieAttack>>, but the << >>syntax reads whatever is inside it as code. You can get very complex with this, and there are certain rules that have to be followed other than just spaces. For now, let's just use the display command inside the << >>.

In my case, I could create a passage with some text like, "You hear a moaning on the wind. Shambling forms come out of the shadows; grabbing hands and rotting flesh are surrounding you and your friends." Instead of repeating the description of a zombie attack every time, I can call up the description. My passage for starting a fire could then look like the example below:

> You burn the books to start a fire. The warmth feels good. You know you can relax for at least this moment.
> <<display ZombieAttack>>
> The library is no longer safe . . .
> Do you grab your stuff and bolt for the [[door| stay in ware-house]] or do you [[Fight it out|Long White Tunnel]]

You might notice that I am reusing passages from before; you can loop people around in circles with these functions.

For this project we also need to call up the catalog. Twine will accept HTML. The game is about using the OPAC, and you can use simple HTML to include it. It would be best to include the call to the catalog in its own passage, so as to use the display command to call it up when necessary.

1. Create a new passage; call it "AccessCatalog."
2. Paste in the code for your catalog; it will look something like this:

```
<iframesrc="http://ibistro.ci.richmond.va.us/uhtbin/cgisirsi/x/0/0/
49" width="600px" height="400px" scrolling="auto" framebor-
der="1"> </iframe>
```

The <br> command is for a line break, so that the IFrame does not cramp any text in your passage. Everything following the "src" inside quotations is the URL of the catalog, its web address. You can simply copy your OPAC's address from the address bar at the top. After you have copied it, place it between the quotation marks and be sure to include the http// or https// of the chunk of code I have given you here.

(The number in the width can be changed to make the display of the OPAC wider, and height can be changed to make it taller. It will have a scroll bar by default. I also included a *frameborder* command so the OPAC stands out more.)

An important note: when players search for resources you will need to give them options about how they found them. If you give a subject-heading search, ask them to go the correct Dewey number; give them wrong options for the search based on keyword or author name or title. For instance, if the player would need to build walls, suggest they subject search "carpenter"; if there is work by Carpenter or the *Karen Carpenter Story* in your collection, include it as an option. If they choose the wrong search, give them a side quest or a feedback page that redirects them to the OPAC until they get it right. *Do not* simply ask if they found the book, because the player can then just say they did and not actually search. Use options that force them to actually search through the OPAC.

6. Collect Graphics and HTML Elements to Put in Your Story

Twine allows you to incorporate HTML. You can use HTML to make fonts bold or italicized and even change their color. One of the more handy uses of HTML is to change the background of a passage using the background command. You can even use it to put images in your pages.

You want to make your searches and pages stimulating, so you could add some pictures of a zombie apocalypse instead of just describing the images. Rather than load up pictures and putting the HTML in to display them, Twine lets us import images through its interface. It will support PNG, GIF, JPEG, WebP, and SVG. The GIFs can be animated for some more fun.

In order to insert images, go to the menu, choose Story, and choose Import Image. You will find two options here. The first is to import an image from a file, and if you have made your own graphics or downloaded images, you can insert them into Twine as simply as attaching a file to an e-mail. You will go to the Story option in the menu, and a menu will drop down. Go to Import Image and select Import from File.

You can also import them from a web page; to do so you will have to find the image online. Right-click the image and copy the URL from the source page. Select Story like before, and when you are prompted from the import for the Web option on the Twine interface, paste the URL into Twine interface. It will save you a step of importing it to your machine.

In either case, it will create a new passage on your Twine screen and you can insert it into an existing passage almost the same way you inserted your other text passages: [img[MyImage]]. In this case, MyImage will be replaced by the name of the image you have downloaded. If you are creating custom images, you may have an easier time modifying some existing graphics to suit your story.

It is also possible to use CSS in Twine. It will let you create a consistent background image, style the pages, and do all the general things that CSS will do to create a web page look. You can do so by right-clicking in the main Twine interface box. The Context menu will pop up and include a new style sheet. All you have to do is select New Style Sheet. One appears in the box, just like a passage. Double-click it and enter CSS. Here are the four main selectors you will have to use.

```
Example selectors: */
body { background-color: White;
/* This affects the entire page */
}
passage { text-color:Black; font-size:1.5 em;
/* This only affects passages */
}
.passage a {
/* This affects passage links */
}
.passage a:hover {
/* This affects links while the cursor is over them */
}
```

There are a lot of tutorials for using CSS if you need support. CSS is not difficult to implement, and you should consider it, if for no other reason than to make an interesting background.

By the same token, Twine will let you insert JavaScript. You could incorporate the code I have given you to share on Facebook in the game. Right-click on the Twine interface and choose New Script Here. You would have to go to the Facebook share/like button generator at https://developers.facebook.com/docs/plugins/share-button and paste the highlighted JavaScript from Facebook in the script window. Enclose the actual HTML inside an <HTML> tag like we did the IFrame.

In this you could let people share they played and won. You can also place a code for awarding a Credly Badge.

Finally, Twine has some of its own pseudo language for making more complicated games. I hope that if you make this game, you will continue to develop it as you get feedback from players. You might find that once you have completed a game, it will be less intimidating to make another one or make your first even better. Your final product could end up with animation, multiple endings, and a sound track.

7. Output from Twine and Find a Hosting Area

Now that you've created your first game, you'll want to put it out there for the world to see. But you'll want to test it first. If you go to Build in the Twine menu, you can choose Verify all Passages to make sure you have not skipped a link or put a "dead link" in your game. After you have made any necessary corrections, you can go to Test Play. It will let you play through your whole game, or you can select a certain passage and play from that point. When you are satisfied with your game, go back to the Build menu one more time and choose Build. Name your file and save wherever you need to save. My suggestion would be to allow some friends or colleagues to try it out once or twice and give you feedback on their experience. Incorporate the feedback you think will be useful and try again with some patrons. Repeat as necessary.

Twine will put out a single file with an HTML extension. The whole game is self-contained on that page and as long as it is on a server. If you have a web page, it can be placed in the Public HTML folder and linked to from another page, or you can load it up to philome.la, a free Twine-hosting page. Philome.la will host your game and give you a URL you can link to from your site. You now have an information literacy video game online. Congratulations on building your first real video game!

GAMIFY LIBRARY ORIENTATION FOR PATRONS WITH A TOP-DOWN VIDEO GAME

This next project can be viewed and played on PlayMyLibrary.me. Play through it to have a better idea of how it's put together. You can also start thinking of your own changes to the project to "make it your own." Feel free to comment.

Video games are an approachable medium for a contemporary audience, and I'm now going to teach *you* how to make one. Technically speaking, this is one of the hardest projects. However, it is based on GameMaker, which is game design software made for users as young as elementary school age. GameMaker has been around for quite some time. It was not something I thought of using for library gamification since it is created to make side-scrollers or top-down games. Games such as *Legend of Zelda, Metron,* and *Super Mario Brothers* do not usually have mechanics that would be considered useful for gamification. Later I saw GameMaker used by VCU's Department of Art Education's CurrentLab to teach middleschool students how to create their own games. Dr. Ryan Patton is the professor who started designing VCU's approach to teaching this game program. It requires the students to make "ethical" games, with "good" not being defined just by shooting the right enemy. Dr. Patton abstractified the game mechanics so that it wasn't simply about shooting but could be about anything and still retain the engaging elements of play. It made me reconsider Game-Maker as a gamification tool for libraries, partially because it is simple to use, but also because it can be customized enough to escape the shooter genre.

Compared to our Twine project, you can create a graphics-based game that has a broad appeal to all game players, including children. The challenge is that while you will be given some basic sprites or character designs, to make this work you will have to play graphic artist. I understand that coding logic and graphic design may be outside your comfort zone, but I will give you specific examples and I believe you will be able to adjust from there. The real difficulty of this project is the same as with every game: you will need to adapt it to your players and your library.

In this chapter I will help you create your player, game space, and an enemy and make them interact. You should pick up some interface logic necessary to create games with GameMaker and maybe a little programming logic. I will give the code you will need to accomplish the tasks in this game and enough explanation so that you understand what you are doing. However, whole books are written about using Game-Maker, so if this is something that you'd like to pursue further beyond this project, please see the resources listed in the "Recommended Readings" chapter.

Game: Legend of Dewey: Quest to Checkout

Objective: Learn what physical areas the library has and what resources are there.

Reward: Entertainment

Mechanics:

1. Download GameMaker and orient yourself to the interface.
2. Understand the mechanics of the game.
3. Create a narrative for the game with villains and objectives.
4. Create the elements of the game: map, objects (walls, player, avoids, bosses, special objects, helpful librarian), and sprites. Place everything in the room.
5. Download the game and place it online or make an app and ask people to share the game.

Gamification Objective: To give the patron a library orientation as well as scope of purpose of the resources in your library and how they can help patrons in life.

GameMaker

GameMaker can be downloaded at https://www.yoyogames.com/studio. You will want to download the free version of GameMaker Studio. It is a Windows program, and for fellow Mac and Linux users, I apologize. There are *paid* versions for both Mac and Windows available. However, my assumption going forward is that you will use the free version.

As a quick orientation to GameMaker, the GameMaker interface looks like this:

The toolbar at the top has all the functions you will be using. Your immediate concern is the left three items on the toolbar: Create a Game, Open a Game, and Save. The first step is to "Create a Game" and name it; the second step is to use the third icon represented by a floppy disk image (which I find ironic since I am unsure if anyone has used a floppy disk in the last twenty years) and save it. Remember to save often! When you go to work on this project, you will use the second icon, "Open a Game," to open it. If you have downloaded the game, you

Figure 5.9.

can move your mouse across the icons and see what they are for. The other icon I will call your attention to is the fourth from the last, called "Game Information." Make sure to fill this out. I know it may seem unnecessary, but it will be useful when you publish your game.

On the left side of the screen, you will see a rather standard folder layout. Whenever you create an object in your game, it will automatically show up in the folder. You may double-click items in that folder structure to reopen them and make changes or edits when applicable.

The other two icons you should familiarize yourself with now are sprites and objects. They have a very special relationship to each other. Every visible item in the game is an object: walls, players, enemies, anything you pick up, and anything you would fire at an enemy or that they would fire at you. When you create an object, like the player, you will give it behaviors, or define how you make it act and how it reacts to other objects in the game. The key to this is that one object can act like many other objects, but they can also look completely different depend-

Figure 5.10.

ing on the situation of the game. The way to change their appearance is to create a "sprite" that you can lay over the "Object": the sprite is how the object looks in the game. More experienced game players will recognize this concept as "a skin."

For those of you who do not know what a skin is, let me give this explanation. You will notice the sprite icon looks like a Pac-Man. Think of the video game *Pac-Man*. Pac-Man looks the same the whole game. He cannot eat the ghosts that are chasing him around the board in his normal state, but after eating a "power pill," he can eat the ghosts. He has the same sprite (appearance) but a different object (function). If Pac-Man were created in GameMaker, he would be two objects, Pac-Man Normal and Pac-Man Powered UP.

The objects have actions. When you have created an object, you will need to add events. When you add an event, you need to go to the right-hand side of the main interface and associate an action with that event. You will notice these actions are on different tabs. I will tell you which tab to go to, but the name of the action will display when you move your mouse over it.

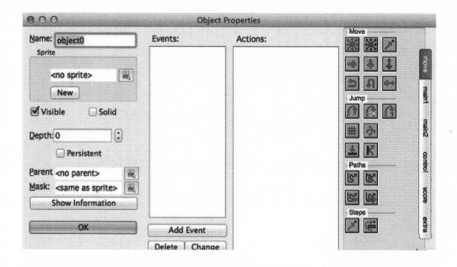

Figure 5.11.

Mechanics of the Game

We are creating what is called a top-down game, not unlike *The Legend of Zelda*. Our game will be called *The Legend of Dewey*. Based on the dynamics of play in those early video games, Dr. Patton made some generalizations that I find useful for starting game design with this interface.

Elements of a Game as Described by Dr. Ryan Patton, VCU

1. Object: an object can be anything, but more importantly it describes how to make a player/boss/wall/ or anything that exists in the game space.
2. Avoid: is an object with negative consequences, usually moving, sometimes not; it is usually generated by a boss or enemy object.
3. Release: is something the player object (or the boss object) generates to have an effect on other objects.
4. Contact: the consequences of two objects meeting.

You will recognize that I have already introduced you to one of the concepts, the object. The next three concepts are how to use objects to create a playable game. If it helps you to think of a shooter game, the players with guns are the objects. The enemy with a gun is an object, but when he shoots, it is considered an *avoid*. When the player shoots, it is a *release*. If the *avoid* hits the player, it is a *contact*. When the player shoots the enemy, it is a contact. If we think of the game in these abstract concepts, we can use the structure and the elements of popular games to learn about library processes and use representations of what every department offers the patron in a more dynamic way.

1. Create a Narrative with Villains Who Can Only Be Beaten by Rewards Gathered from Each Section

The first part of this process is to create your narrative. Now remember, this is not a story necessarily as in the Twine game. Instead, we are creating a framework for the game mechanics. The story is simple enough. A player goes to the library and beats the bosses, using the tools each department provides. The gamified objective is to make them conscious of each department and more importantly its value.

Here is where you can describe the sections of the library and what their "value" is to the patrons. Change the bosses and rewards for each section if you disagree with my assumptions.

1. Children's: Literacy
2. Reference: Information Literacy
3. Fiction: Civilized
4. Media: Social Awareness
5. Activity Room: Social
6. Periodicals: Contemporary Knowledge
7. Computer Lab: Digital Literacy

Using the value I decided upon, create ideal enemies for each section and a special power you can pick up from each section:

1. Children's: Mr. JibberJabber/Literature Light
2. Reference: Hoodwink Helen and Her Hoax Bombs/Fact Fan
3. Fiction: Barbaric Bob/The Civil Salvo
4. Media: Retro Rod/Current Cry
5. Activity Room: Introverted Ivan/Neighborly Net
6. Periodicals: Antique Amy/Mod Squad

7. Computer Lab: General Ludd/Geek Speak

Now we can create the elements of the game as we have a framework for the narrative to use in guiding us.

2. Create a Map of the Library, Designating Each Section You Want the Player to Visit

The first thing we need is a space where the game takes place. There is some math involved here, and you will probably have to fudge the specs a little. I explained earlier how to find a map of your library; notice that somewhere on the map of the library is an interior door. The standard size for an interior door is 32 inches. The default size of a player in GameMaker is 32 x 32 pixels. If you are tempted to create yours 32 pixels wide and work out your specs from there, don't. If you do that, your player will get stuck when he tries to pass through the doors, so the smallest door must be 64 pixels wide. That means our player is very skinny.

1. Measure the smallest door on the map.
2. Divide all the other measurements by the width of that door. (Here is where you can fudge a little. If your door is an inch wide and the whole building on the map is 24 and 1/16, just make it 24 and a 1/2.)
3. If the side of your building is 84 feet and the door is 32 inches, the result would be 31.5.
4. Now you have to multiply that by 64.
5. The result is 2,016.
6. The front of your building is 50 feet— divide by 32.
7. Now you have to multiply that by 64.
8. The front of the building is 1,200.
9. If your building is irregular or there are nonpublic spaces that increase the measurement, you should omit them from the map and base your measurements on the omissions.

When you create a room, it will be 2,016 pixels by 1,200 pixels. To do this, look on the top icon menu in the GameMaker interface window.

Select the Create Room icon; it looks like a little white box with a blue border.

You will get a pop-up window. You will notice there a series of tabs directly under the menu on the left. These are very important to the game. We will be returning to them from time to time. Choose the second tab and enter your generated measurements for the room: 2,016 pixels by 1,200 pixels.

This room is huge and may be larger than your screen. To make sure it is playable, you need to do the next step. Click the small arrow next to the button under the toolbar until you get the view "option showing." Select "enable view zero" then select "visible" when room starts; for the selection *object following*, choose your player. I know it seems anticlimactic to move on at this point, but we need something to place in the

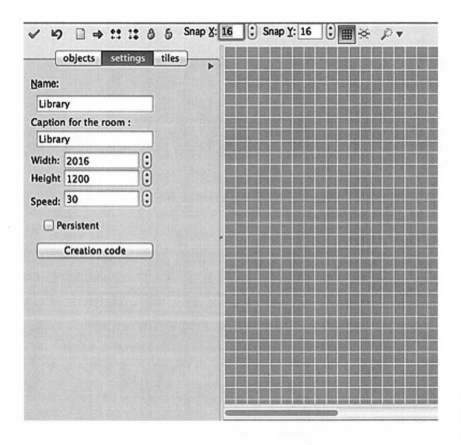

Figure 5.12.

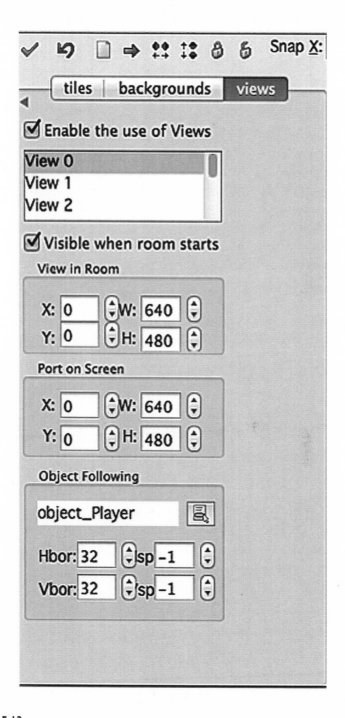

Figure 5.13.

room. We will have to create our objects and make them visible. We will return to this screen later at the end of the instructions. Click the green check mark and move on.

3. Create Objects

Now for the fun part! You actually get to play game designer and make objects that actually function. A word of warning though: you will be making a large number of objects, and you need to remember to re-name them. The first rule of coding is *stay organized* and comment. You are coding in this program, even though you are using an interface to do so. Renaming each object will serve as your comments. You do not need to discourage yourself by not remembering if the chair was object 16 or object17, or if the second wall you made is *Object_Wall* or *Object_Wall2*.

Creating Walls

Since it has no real actions, we can start with a wall. Click on the Create Object icon in the GameMaker interface: it looks like a blue ball. You will immediately see a window pop up; also of importance is the object created in the file structure on the right side of the main GameMaker interface. It will appear as Object1. You will notice a small check box on the left side labeled Solid. Make sure to *check* this and then you will rename this name *Object_Wall*.

A wall does nothing, but it is the only thing in a room. Is the outside of your building one solid wall? To make it more realistic, do you need windows? Do you have desks, computer stations, and bookshelves? I mention these examples for a reason. They are all objects that do nothing but sit there. They are also objects your character cannot go through.

Go to the GameMaker main screen:

- Select the Objects file structure.
- Either right-click and create a group or go to the main GameMaker menu and choose Edit to create a group.
- Call it Group_Solid.
- Drag and drop the *Object_Wall* in the group.

- Now you can duplicate the wall object by right-clicking on it and choosing Duplicate.
- When you duplicate it, it will appear in the group.
- Double-click it to open it; notice it is already checked solid.
- Name it *Object_Window*.
- Now make *Object_Wall* the parent of object window.
- By choosing Parent, every command that effects the *Object_Wall* will affect the *Object_Window*.
- Now duplicate *Object_Window* and make an *Object_Bookshelf*.
- Every duplicate of *Object_Window* will have *Object_Wall* as its parent.

Later you will just assign a new sprite to these items. Now you have a series of objects you can place to stop the player inside the room.

Creating the Player Object

Use what you have learned already to make an *Object_Wall* to make an Object Player1. Do *not* select solid. This is an object that actually does something. You will need to notice two boxes, one-named *events* and another named *actions*. If you press the button Add Event, another pop-up will appear.

First you want to tell The Player how to move.

- Select is the keyboard button (you can also use Key Press).
- Select <LEFT>.
- You will now notice it appears in the events window above.
- Click Move Fixed symbol on the left.
- Drag that symbol over to the Actions section.
- A new screen will open with options for how the character will move.
- On the top is an option marked *applies to*; the default for this is SELF—remember this: it will be important for other commands.
- Click on the arrow pointing *left* (see the correlation?) and set your speed to 15.
- Click the button on the bottom marked OK, and it is saved in the object.
- Now repeat those steps for right, up, and down, choosing the appropriate direction from Move Fixed.

You have added four events to your player and assigned actions to them. Your character will now move as the keyboard is pressed; however, he will not stop. The player will keep moving in one direction unless you tell it to stop. Now you need to add events for stopping.

You will chose to add the same instructions with either Keyboard or Key Press, but choose the <No Key> option under the choices and again add the start moving button; now set motion to the center button with a speed of 0.

Basically you told the game that when no key is pressed, your character would stop running. Now you have a movable character that will stand still when you tell it to.

We need to make some constraints on the character's motion. If the player can't walk through walls, the next thing to do is add a collision statement.

- Again chose Add Event.
- Now choose Collision from the drop-down menu. It is two red arrows pointing at each other.
- Notice when you choose Collision that all the objects you made appear in a new drop-down.
- Go to the Group Solid and choose *Object_Wall*.
- You will again choose the red Move button, and select the center for stop.
- Speed should be 0.

Now all the items in that group have *Object_Wall* set as their parent. The collision with object wall now affects its *children*, so by selecting *Object_Wall*, you have chosen all those items and keep them straight by confining them in the Group Solid.

Creating Avoids

The villain will make something to avoid. You might wonder why I am not creating the villain first, but that will be explained in time. Now go to Create Object and name him *Object_Avoid*. We know how to do that.

1. Create an object called an *Avoid*.
2. Add an event Create and make the action move toward a point.

3. Type in under X co-ordinate: *Object_Player1*.x.
4. Type in under Y co-ordinate: *Object_Player1*.y.
5. Set the speed to slightly faster than your player (if your player speed was 15, make it 18).
6. Add an event collision.
7. Choose *Object_Wall* for the collision.
8. Go to the left tabs again and choose Main1.
9. Select Destroy the Instance and drag and drop it in the events box.
10. Make sure Self is selected in Destroy the Instance box.
11. Now go back to add event and choose Other; it looks like a green diamond.
12. Now choose Views, and in that pop-up, choose Outside View0; remember that it was that view that followed the player.
13. Create another Destroy the Instance just like the last.
14. Finally add event collision with *Object_Player1* and again destroy instance.

The Move Toward command is making the object aimed at the player, which is controlled by the string after x. Now you can duplicate those objects for each boss; we will make the first duplicate a child of the first *Avoid*. You will name the *Object_Avoid1*, *Object_Avoid2*, and so on, until you have as many avoids as bosses. When you do change the speed, make it a little faster for each *Avoid*. If you make them a little faster—for instance, if our first speed was16, next try 18, and so on—to increase the difficulty.

Creating the Boss Object

Starting with Mr. JibberJabber, our bad guy, this boss will follow the player around and release *Avoids* at the player; create a new object and name him *Object_Boss*.

In the Object _Boss we need to set up some actions:

- Select Add Event from the menu.
- Go the tabs on the right and under the Move Tab, choose the one marked Step Avoiding.
- Add Step Avoiding and a pop-up screen will appear.
- You need to add these lines to the box.

- Under x: Object_Player.x.
- Under y: Object Player.y.
- Speed:8.
- Leave solid only on the bottom box.
- Click on the Control tab on the right and choose Test Chance.
- Type "20" in the box marked Sides.
- Next go to Main1 and drag the Create Instance.
- Check *Applies To*: Other.
- In the box marked *Object*, you will chose Object_Avoid.
- Click the relative.

The boss now follows the player because his motion is set to Step Avoiding and Object+Player is the co-ordinate set. (You know you created two Object_Players, correct? The boss must be set to Step Avoiding the first player, not the second. The second object player is in a different state.) The Test Chance means that every 20 turns, which there are 30 by default in a room, the program will randomly decide to create an *Avoid*. Now duplicate the boss and make the duplicates children like before. Double-click each boss in turn, and make the number in the Test Chance dialog box smaller. Now change the *create instance* in the bosses' actions to the corresponding *Avoids*: *Object_Boss1* creates *Object_Avoid1*, etc. You did check Relative in the create boxes, right? If not, the item created will be not be *relative* to the object creating it: in this case the *Avoid* would not come from the *Object_Boss*; instead, it will generate at the 0,0 position of the map. If you have done as I suggest, you should now have bosses that shoot progressively faster objects and shoot them more often. So you have increased the difficulty of each boss for the player.

The Librarian: Our NPC

We need a way to give the player commands and orient them to the game. We are going to create an NPC, or nonplayer character. They are usually a way to get hints and add exposition to the game.

- First create an Object.
- Name it *Object_Librarian*.
- Select Add Event from the menu.

- Choose the Step Avoiding like you did with the boss, and make the x and y co-ordinates object_player same as the boss.
- Now *add_Event* collision and choose player.
- Choose Start a Block under the Control tab.
- On the main2 tab of the interface under info is Display Message.
- In the pop-up, you will write something like "Welcome to the library; we have many resources, etc. Beware of Mr. JibberJabber; he makes no sense."
- Add Create Instance on tab 2 and create a copy of librarian and call it *object_ librarian_B*.
- Add a Destroy the Instance and effect *self*.
- Add a Create Instance and add the object_boss.
- Choose End Block on control tab.

Now for librarian B: this librarian will not move, only display a message, so you may copy the object_librairian_. Simply remove the first event that adds action and omit the next two commands. Keep the same sprite.

- Add Event Create and choose Set Alarm from timing on the Control tab.
- Set the number of steps on Alarm to 90; that is 3 seconds.
- Now Add Event Alarm0, or if you set the Alarm to something other than zero, use that number.
- Add create_instance and choose Object boss. (When you have made a librarian B for each boss, you will change this to the appropriate one.)
- Now change the collision event for the Object_Player and add a message to explain about that boss.

At this point you want to duplicate the librarian; make as many librarians as you have bosses. Under each librarian, change the text warning and Create Instance to the corresponding boss and Change the Display Message to reflect the new boss.

Special Objects

The bosses must be defeated, of course. The player will need special objects to gather from around the library to defeat them. You want to make special objects to do this. The object will just tell what it is unless the boss is available; then it will change your player into a super-powered player.

- First create an object.
- Call it *Object_Special1*.
- Use add events to create collision with Object_Player.
- Add Display a Message, and use it to explain what the object is.
- Go to the Control tab and drag and drop Check_Instance to actions.
- For the object dialog choose *Object_Boss1*; change each power up to reflect their bosses.
- For the number dialog set it to 1. This means an object will only power up the player when the right boss is on the screen.
- Choose a start step block from the Control tab.
- Go to main1 tab and add Change_Sprite and choose the *Object_Player*.
- You will make a special powered-up sprite for this and select to change it to sprite_player_powered.
- On the main2 tab of the interface, under info, is Display Message.
- Write some text telling the player by which object they are now super powered.
- Choose Set Variable from Variables under Control tab.
- Apply this to object player, name your variable player, and set it to 1; when the player has a player variable of one, it will affect things differently.
- Now return to Control and bring over the end block.
- Next add the Jump to Position from the Move tab, and under x add +120; make sure to click Relative, so the special object will move when you hit it.

Now we need to add some code to Object_Player1.

- Chose Create from the Add Event.
- On the Score menu, add Set the Health; give your player a value of 150.
- Add Set_Variable from the Control tab, name the variable Player, and set it to 2.
- Add event collision with *Object_Avoid*.

STEP-BY-STEP LIBRARY PROJECTS FOR GAMIFICATION   111

- Add Test_Variable to the event; in the variable box put player, and for value put 1.
- Put Reverse Direction Next from the Move tab; apply to other.
- Next place an Else Action from the Control tab in this event.
- For the next action choose Set Health: give a factor of -10, and click Relative.

Player One will now take damage from the avoids! Or if he has touched the right special object, the avoids will bounce off him!

Now, we need to make the player super powered if he meets the boss.

Return to the Boss Object.

- Add Event Collision with Object_player.
- Again Add Event Check Variable from Control, make it other, and see if player is at 1.
- Add the Start Step from Control tab.
- Add the event *Destroy_instance* and choose Self.
- Add Change Sprite and choose object_player and change the sprite to sprite_player.
- Add *change_instance* from objects under Main tab2; change the object_librarianB to the object_librarian2 (you will change these so each boss progresses to each stage).
- Add *set_variable*, choose other or object, and make the object *Object_player*; name it Player and make it 2 again.
- Now choose End Step Block from Control tab.
- Next add an Else statement.
- Add Jump to random position from the Move tab.
- Make it affect the player.

Now your boss will knock the player to a random position if he touches him, unless he is in the powered phase; then he will be destroyed.

- On the same tab as Create Health is Test Health; drag it to the actions. The pop-up will have 0 as a value to test for; let that remain.
- Click Relative (now the player's health bar will follow him around).
- Next choose Control tab above the Score tab.

- Chose Start Block and drag it to Actions; you will notice that it is indented compared to the test health. This means it is only taking action when health is zero (now you're learning to program).
- Next, on the Main1 tab, chose the Change Sprite icon; just let it be, since we have not made sprites yet.
- Next, above Change Sprite is Destroy the Instance; drag that under the Change Sprite, and choose *Object_Avoid1*.
- Go to the Move tab on the right.
- Choose Jump to Random, apply to object, choose *Object_Boss1*.
- Next go to the Main2 tab.
- Choose Set Alarm and set it for 60.
- Under that, place Reset Health and put it back to 100.
- Finally, go back to Control tab and choose End of Block.
- Add events and choose Alarm0.
- Now place the action change sprite and choose Sprite 1.

The final step is to make a health bar. Create an object called Object_health.

- *Add Event* Step.
- For the action put jump to position.
- Make the position X equal object_player.x and Y equal object_player.y.
- Add event Draw.
- On the Score tab on the far left side, chose Set Health.
- Now choose Draw Health Bar.
- Set the values for the health bar at X1:-20 Y1:-35 X2:20 Y2:-30. Click Relative.

Place this object in the room, and it will follow the player; make sure the player sprite is "Centered."

4. Create or Design Characters

The problem you have now is that you have objects, but even if you make a room, they look like nothing. Remember the object–sprite relationship? You will need to create characters for your game. To create a sprite, let us start with an easy one, the wall.

First, click on Create Sprite in the toolbar; remember, it looks like a red Pac-Man. This is the screen you will see. On the left side you have two choices: load or edit. For the wall, we will edit. Do *not* change the setting on anything else. Click on Edit Sprite, which takes you to this screen. You will notice that it is called Image Zero; do not rename it, just double-click on image0, and go into the graphic editor. We will explain why it is called Image Zero later.

When the box is open, you have some very basic tools for creating an image. They are similar to the Microsoft Paint program that is standard in Windows. If you do not know how to use the tools in front of you, do not be too concerned; that is why there is the Load Image command. However, there will be an occasion where you will load an image and want to change something. You can do it through this screen. Then you will use the same steps for creating a sprite for a wall later to make a window sprite or a bookshelf sprite or anything you don't want your character to go through.

Tip: You might notice when you go to display a block like this, one whole color is gone; for a wall you can uncheck the transparency button, and the whole image will show. If you want to keep transparency, or create an image with transparency instead of just a big block, check the color in the bottom left corner of the editor. Whatever color is in that corner chooses a transparency, and anything that color in your image will not show in the game.

At this point you might be thinking, "Wow, that is a lot of work if I have to make a character. I am not an artist." So feel free to Google images of your character or use one of the avatar generators. There are

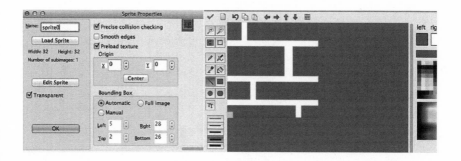

Figure 5.14.

also some great free resources for images for games in the "Tools and Applications" chapter. The player is set by default to a height and width of 32 x 32 pixels. You will have to scale it down to that size with whatever image you choose. Along with image editors you can use, all are in the "Tools and Applications" section of this book.

Let me explain why Image Zero is important. There is also the ability to load an animated GIF. If you understand what an animated GIF is, good. If not, it is a kind of moving image. It moves by combining multiple images in one file and cycling through them. If you want a more interesting game, you can load one, and you will see every image listed in order when you edit a sprite.

If you choose to download an image or an animated GIF, you still need to edit to be the correct size. If it is an animated GIF, correct the size *before* you load it; if you try to load the GIF and reload image 0, it will be changed independently of image 1. Each image can be edited individually. That also means you can Copy Image 1 and make changes to the copy and create your own animation.

Once you have a sprite, you can duplicate it: call it Sprite_Player_shocked.

- Double-click Sprite_Player_shocked.
- Click Edit Sprite.
- On the top menu of the sprite editor are copy and paste icons.
- Click Copy and Paste.
- Now you have Image 0 *and* Image1.
- Click Image1.
- Draw little lightning bolts or Zs on it.
- Click the green check mark in the upper right corner.

You have now saved and animated a GIF of your player when he is shocked by the avoids. Remember the Change Sprite Command I did not fully explain for Player_Object1?

Go back to Player_Object1. Assign the Sprite Player to the Object_Player1. Now go into the Step Command and find the step that looks like a red Pac-Man. You have two. For the first one, change the sprite to sprite_player_shocked. Use your sprite for the player where you had added little lightning bolts or Zs.

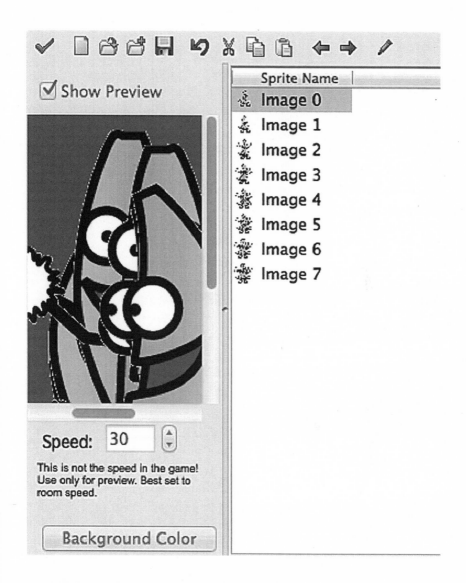

Figure 5.15.

You can play with the timing by copying the images. If you copy the one you added Zs to, it will cycle through, and the second image will last longer; you can also create a third image or a fourth.

When your player is dazed, he will look like he is dazed. You can do similar things for the contact of avoids or even use this to make walk cycles. There are some open-source graphics for explosions and such in the resources section.

5. Place Everything in the Room

Select your *Object_Wall* and place it all around the room. First go to the lower left-hand corner, and GameMaker has a nice list of all the available objects. Choose *Object_Wall* and place it around the edges of the screen; these are your exterior walls. If you need to make a long run, right-click the mouse; every block you drag it across will now have the selected object in it. You have now created your first room.

Now you can create objects inside the room. Remember for the purposes of this game, anything inside that is not something to pick up can stop the player. Your map should give you dimensions of your windows and how to calculate them from the door sizes. It might be advisable to go back and make sprites for all the interior objects that you need. You can then place them throughout the library based on your map. What if you need a desk and it is four times the size of the door? Create a sprite for it; this time make your sprite 64 x 4 or 256 pixels wide by 265 pixels long. Sprites are related to objects, but the size of an object is set by the sprite size in pixels, not the size of the actual object. Of course, you will want to stay as true to the actual layout of your library as possible.

The other thing you will need to do is place your player object by the doors of the library. It is often overlooked that if you do not place your character in a room, they will not be available to play. You will also need to place the librarian in the room. Options for making the librarian move are available in the references in my "Tips and Tricks" section.

You could, at this point, save the room and, using the green arrow at the top on the main toolbar, play the room (even with nothing in it). However, the room is huge and may be larger than your screen. To make sure it is playable, you need to do the next step.

- A small arrow is next to the button under the toolbar.
- Click that button until you get the view "option showing."
- Select enable view zero.
- Select visible when room starts.
- For the selection Object Following, choose your player.

Now play the room and make sure walls stop your character and also make sure the motion works properly.

Let me guess: it didn't work, right? Well, that is part of the process. I test ran this myself. I know that the steps I gave you work. However, it is a lot of information to deal with and you're sure to overlook something. Even more importantly, this is part of the process of making a game; you are your first test audience. I have some extra steps for you at the end of this chapter, but right now learn to debug. If you try more of these, it will serve you well.

You might be disappointed by how the dialog boxes look or think it would be better to shoot the bosses. Maybe you want to add hidden objects or use the bookshelf sprite on an object that would call up a dialog box about a book in that section. There are more resources for changing the game when you feel ready.

6. Download the Game or Make It an App

If you have saved your game, it is playable by anyone with GameMaker on his or her computer. This will not do us much good as librarians. The GameMaker Studio can be bought for roughly $20; GameMaker has a publishing option. It will allow you to post it to a website as an HTML5 game. For a little more, you can even export it as an Android app. You simply need to make a web version and include the share function or put a Credly Code. If you are running a blog section, let players comment and try to correct on their suggestions.

Now the interesting thing about this is that you might have noticed some pro options not available to you. One of these is the ability to load a URL inside the *game* so that you can share or add badges as each objective for each department is met. One of the more interesting things you could do is make the hidden objects I suggested, such as catalog entries or a book description that has the same sprite as bookshelves that would activate when you trip a collision event. Then let players share that they found a hidden object or "Easter egg" as they're called in games.

Another element to add is points; you can create a scoreboard and remove points from it as the time goes on. You will find resources for creating points and leaderboards and scores in the resources section. Indeed, there are many things you can do; instead of placing special objects, you can hide them in books and create counts for finding three of them before getting the power. If this sounds difficult, there is a strong GameMaker community too, and some of them may be willing to help you. They may even have a full version of the software, and be willing to take your file and export an Android version for you! After a while, you may, like me, find making video games a bit of an addiction.

6

TIPS AND TRICKS

EASTER EGGS

The entire gamified catalog or Clandestine Catalog project was based around the concept of "Easter eggs." Historically, they have been in video games since the late 1970s and reportedly originated with Atari. Often, Easter eggs are a secret message or special power, which can only be unlocked by doing something that was not part of the stated game objectives. You saw this incorporated in games later as hidden levels or hidden power-ups.

I suggested that you include several Easter eggs in your games, like the Gamified Staff Orientation or the Gamified Library Orientation. I think the Gamified OPAC has the opportunity to make an even better game, with a secondary mission built into it. For example, if a character chooses a specific book, you could send them to find a local author with special knowledge of your area. I understand that I can't cover all the possibilities of the interfaces I suggested to make the games, but many of these allow a great opportunity for Easter eggs. The more obscure or specific to your area, or your library, the better the Easter egg would be.

Even the Clandestine Catalog, which is an Easter egg hunt across the city, could have an Easter egg. Remember Aurasma will alert you to a nearby Aura. What if you had used signs up to that point and created an Aura without the sign as a trigger image? Maybe use a local land-mark? Their phone would tell them there was an Aura nearby, but they would have to find what triggers it, maybe just a simpler logo on a building or landmark instead of whatever trigger image you had used up until that point.

The main reason for Easter eggs is, for those who discover the hidden reward, it is satisfying in a different way than just winning. The player is rewarded for not playing the same way everyone else does. It is a different area of competition and a new way to play. It also can help to prolong a game. Instead of losing players who quickly run through all of the options in a game or think they have won it once already, Easter eggs may bring them back to see if they missed anything. Someone who discovers an Easter egg in a game can show the other players who did not think it challenging that there may be more to the game than they thought and reinforce its use. For an ongoing gamification, individual games can get old quickly and you risk losing your players. To stay current, create a few Easter eggs to introduce new elements and get players back who have left.

USE FEEDBACK FROM PLAYERS

"You can please some of the people all of the time; you can please all of the people some of the time; but you can't please all of the people all of the time" is the famous quote by John Lydgate, but to be honest, we are usually lucky to please some of the people some of the time. So keep changing it up; if someone doesn't like an aspect of your game, feel free to change that aspect of the game. There is every possibility that what you change will be something somebody else liked. It is not a problem though; you can change it back or try and ask the player what he or she liked about it that another player didn't, and if relevant try something new. I understand that time is a challenge for library staff, and libraries are not likely to have someone dedicated to making games. However, it is not a bad idea to keep that feedback channel open. Making a change, and ideally advertising it to users periodically, will only help justify your original investment of time.

DON'T MAKE YOUR OWN GRAPHICS UNLESS YOU WANT TO

There are many available resources for graphics for your games. I covered some in the Tools and Applications part of the book. Some of the tools you have or were shown can modify graphics as well as create them. If you don't have Photoshop, iPiccy, PhotoCat, and other online image editing software can be used to do many of the things that Photoshop can. You can use Google and use search tools to look for images under "free to use with modification" or "free to use for noncommercial purposes" under usage rights. It will allow you to use web images as long as they are under a creative commons license and you give credit to the originator of the images.

In many cases the artist would probably be very happy to see their work used by someone, but make sure to give out their contact information. There are many talented artists who would love to get more exposure by way of your usage, including people making animations for games. It might even be worth talking to the artist about using their work and having them modify images for you. And don't discredit what clout your library may have in the community. To some artists the opportunity to help make a project that the *library* will use and that they can include in their portfolio may be enough to reason to do the work for free, which leads to my next point.

DON'T BE AFRAID TO ASK FOR HELP

There are strong user communities built around game design programs and open badges. The resources section in this book will give you message boards and threads on game design. Visit them; you may see an idea you can use. There are sites where indie game developers show off what they have made. You might see a game that could be modified for your purposes. I encourage you to reach out and ask them how they did it. Most game designers love to talk about how they did something particularly clever or help others do it. Many of the people working in some of the interfaces I used for the projects are doing so out of passion for the medium. I received aid from local game designers, and yours would probably be as happy to help.

The same thing goes for other librarians. I know in many cases these kinds of projects are a hard sell to some more traditional staff. Those are the people to ask for help though. They might not be willing to help but their reasons why might be useful. Once, I asked some librarians about the Aurasma project and was told their patronage did not have smartphones. I thought about that and realized that versions of the games can be made with just a sign and a number to text. Make a number with an auto response from a Google Voice account and auto reply from an e-mail. Sometimes the people who protest something as useless can also give you the best ideas for creating other options that might not be as "cool" but will still achieve your objective, which is also my final point.

DON'T BE SEDUCED BY THE COOL

I admit that I was first attracted to using games in libraries because they were cool, interesting, and fun. There is definitely a cool factor to the idea of gamifying something, but we need to do it in moderation. You will have many ideas for new elements to add, but focus on the objective of teaching a lesson, get that down, and improve later. If you shoot for everything, you will miss most of it. There are certainly arguments to be made for gamifying library processes, but let's also take small steps and control what we can do. You want moderate success at first, so do the easiest thing you can. Then make a list of how you would like to modify them and check them off one at a time. Particle animations, multiplayer scenarios, or anything else you can think of might be a great idea, but implementing them might take time and resources you don't have. In production we used to call this going down the rabbit hole. Don't get so obsessed with one particular idea that you lose sight of the whole picture.

7

FUTURE TRENDS

What is the future of gamification? Even though Gartner predicted that there would be "70 percent of Global 2000 businesses managing at least one 'gamified' application or system by 2014," we are already seeing some of the shine wear off this technology.[1] Gartner research VP Brian Burke was quoted in TechCrunch as saying: "I'm positive on gamification overall, but as the tech gets hyped there are a lot of misled expectations on what can be achieved. People are just doing it badly. You can't just put badges on something and expect it to work."[2] Gamification has a lot of hype and interest but that is because of people being interested in what it can deliver, not how it can deliver it.

Foursquare, the long-term leader in gamification, dropped a lot of its gamification element in 2014 from the Foursquare app. It was not because the gamification elements were not popular; rather, the fact was that their implementation was failing. It had to drop the gamified elements from Foursquare because they were too successful. After a certain point, new players simply could not compete with established players and it was not "fun" for either. The new players could never become "Mayor" of a location no matter how many times they checked in, and the established players were no longer challenged. Foursquare was losing players and so it adapted. It relaunched the Mayorships in a new app called Swarm. Now instead of competing with everyone, you can compete with your circle of friends. It is demonstrative of what makes gamification powerful and at the same time so hard to implement properly. For gamification to work, it has to be fun and continue to provide challenges.

I specifically chose to focus on several different projects, many of them not actually considered gamification. I chose more serious games because they teach us that how you play is where the fun in games comes from, not the lesson. The games themselves need to be fun, and not having that element is what is causing failure in gamification systems. We often get caught up in the external parts of gamification without understanding how it is really operating. Refer to my examples about how the mechanics of a game create the challenges and then the engagement; gamification is not a one-size-fits-all proposition. Sometimes, gamification turns out to be bad for organizations because they are trying to turn something not fun into fun simply by adding badges. When organizations do not provide a challenge that is fun to overcome, the reward becomes meaningless.

It is reminiscent of the move toward social media not that long ago. A couple of years ago everyone was talking about how social media would help engage the millennials. People are still trying to get it right and we saw too few successes. People were focusing on it as print medium advertising services, instead of establishing entertaining content for followers to have conversation over, in effect losing the whole "social" part of the media. Social media works when you get your users to have the conversation for you, not when you do the talking. They missed the point of what made social media work. In a similar vein, I think the future of gamification will depend on us letting the players tell us what are "fun" games, not simply using BPL to promote our services and needs.

What does that mean for libraries and gamification? Well, we are discovering it now. LemonTree and OrangeTree of LibraryGame have opened themselves to new users; Chicago's Summer of Learning used open badges in 2013; the ALA YA committee is exploring open badges for ongoing efforts; and the U.S. Department of Education, NPR, and NASA all use open badges. And in February 2014 OCLC was starting to explore badging on WebJunction. The question is not if we will be gamifying the library experience but if we will be doing it well.

Does this mean that gamification is not worth pursuing right now? No, not at all. I think that we will see a big spike and a lot of bad attempts at doing it but a few good ones, like Ann Arbor's "The Summer Game." The good ones will grow and people will start having conversations beyond BPL and start to really look at the idea of "fun" in learning. Even the bad attempts are going to help us learn how to gamify processes. AADL's Eli Neiburger admitted that not everything they tried worked in "The Summer Game." Remember the words of Thomas Edison: "I haven't failed; I have just learned ten thousand ways that will not work." Every attempt will give you a piece of that puzzle and you'll learn what works for your patrons. We just have to know that we have to make mistakes, one size does not fit all, and most importantly to have fun doing it. Fun is what gamification is about, yours and the players.

NOTES

1. Brian Burke, "Innovation Insight: Gamification Adds Fun and Innovation to Inspire Engagement," December 20, 2011, https://www.gartner.com/doc/1879916/innovation-insight-gamification-adds-fun.

2. Ingrid Lunden, "Badges Beware: 80% Of Gamification Apps Will End Up Being Losers, Says Gartner," TechCrunch, November 27, 2012, http://techcrunch.com/2012/11/27/badges-beware-80-of-gamification-apps-will-end-up-being-losers-says-gartner/ (retrieved November 9, 2014).

RECOMMENDED READINGS AND RESOURCES

BOOKS—GENERAL

Here is a list of books that have served to inform the study of gamification.

McGonigal, J. (2011). *Reality Is Broken: Why Games Make Us Better and How They Can Change the World*. New York: Penguin Press. *Reality Is Broken* is not a book about gamification. It is about serious games, but I still think it is one the most important of the books in this list. Part of the larger issue with gamification, as I stated in the last chapter, is whether it will prove to be a useful tool and can make the connection between your audience, fun in the gameplay, and behavioral goals. Serious games are the framework where you can discover the connection between entertainment and thinking differently about games.

Gee, J. (2003). *What Video Games Have To Teach Us about Learning and Literacy*. New York: Palgrave Macmillan. Again, this work is not about gamification; it is about how teaching is done by games. It is a theoretical versus a practical guide on how we can approach learning through gameplay, how games teach, and most importantly how learning from games is carried over into the players' actual life. The book illustrates how games are problem-solving exercises and why that approach is how they are successful at teaching. It is also a good basis for understanding video game development for those who do not have a related knowledge.

Werbach, K., and D. Hunter. (2012). *For the Win: How Game Thinking Can Revolutionize Your Business*. Philadelphia: Wharton Digital Press. The book most cited as the definitive text on gamification, if such a text exists at this point, is *For the Win*. Defined by its purpose to make more efficient businesses based on the technologic environment that many millennial and digital natives grew up in, it still has lessons for the nonprofit about employee and patron engagement. Ken Werbach is considered one of the leaders in the promotion of gamification; he also is the "instructor" for a Coursera class on the subject. I would strongly suggest his work since it is geared to showing a calculable return on your efforts, versus the more abstract social returns of the previous texts.

Bartle, R. (2009). *Beyond Game Design: Nine Steps Towards Creating Better Videogames*. Boston, MA: Charles River Media/Cengage Technology. The book is included because gamification comes from good games. Richard Bartle is really the first game designer to move out of design into an academic framework. The Bartle player types are the basis of many gamification designs. It is a collection of essays that address the larger question of a game player's motivations and how to address them from a design point of view.

Csikszentmihalyi, M. (2014). *Flow*. New York: HarperCollins e-Books. Not the easiest read in the world and not necessarily a practical guide to understanding how to gamify something, but it is the first work to address the elements of play that engage people. I include it because the better your grounding in the theoretical framework gamification exists in, the easier it will be to understand how to do it well. You should not neglect this book.

Habgood, J., and M. Overmars. (2006). *The Game Maker's Apprentice: Game Development for Beginners*. Berkeley, CA: Apress. If you get to a point in GameMaker where you feel you would like to develop more, *The Game Maker's Apprentice* is one of the better texts to understand that particular program. There are other books on this subject, but this one in general seems to be the one that is most commonly referred to on the boards for beginners. I would not consider it the definitive text but this and its follow-up book, *The Game Maker's Companion*, are two works for help in using the GameMaker interface.

WEBSITES

http://www.pixelprospector.com/. The website is full of resources for designing video games and good games in general. It would be worth your time to see what others have developed and the general state of indie game development. It is also a good resource for seeing what single individuals without development teams are capable of creating.

http://www.gamasutra.com/. More of an industry site than Pixel Prospector, it still has many articles about the practice and theory of game design. You will find articles mentioned in this text here, including this one: http://www.gamasutra.com/view/feature/132341/the_13_ basic_principles_of_.php.

http://currentlab.art.vcu.edu/game-design-cards/If you need some easy shortcuts for modifying your GameMaker project, Dr. Ryan Patton and several of his students have put together some resource cards for creating common game elements. They are easier than reading the GameMaker books and available for free.

http://opengameart.org/. Likewise, if you find yourself in need of some game art for any of the projects, this website is full of Creative Commons and freely shared pixel art that can be included in your games.

MOOCS AND MESSAGE BOARDS

https://www.coursera.org/course/gamificationIf you want a larger overview of this field, there is a Coursera course available occasionally on gamification taught by Ken Werbach of the University of Pennsylvania.

http://twinery.org/wiki/twine_referenceIf you have any question about how Twine works or need help, this discussion board is very useful. By the time you're reading this, a new version of the program may be available.

http://gmc.yoyogames.com/. Likewise, YoYoGames hosts an open chat board for GameMaker users. While it can be helpful for finding out how to do a specific action you envision, be warned: GameMaker has its own special programming language; most of the people on this board will be using the more sophisticated language versus the drag-and-drop interface taught in this work.

VIDEOS

http://www.ted.com/talks/tom_chatfield_7_ways_games_reward_the_brain. A Ted Talk video available online is a good resource to better understand how games work in rewarding the player.

http://codingconduct.cc/Meaningful-Play. The video is an hour summary of good game design and gamification from Google's Tech Talk series.

https://www.youtube.com/watch?v=F4YP-hGZTuA. Amy Jo Kim talks about how to apply game design principles to games and gamification. Not geared toward specifically gamifying an activity, it talks about the larger context of playing online and keeping people engaged.

INDEX

ABOUT THE AUTHOR

David Folmar is the emerging technology librarian at Richmond Public Library. He is an MLS, CTS, and CSM. He sits on the RVA Maker-Fest Leadership Committee and is directly involved in his community's CoderDojo, indie game development, and independent filmmaking community. David is new to librarianship but has a previous career in audiovisual production and digital communications. David looks for the areas where community engagement, STEAM education, social reasonability, and technology overlap.

Originally from Pennsylvania and once having studied at the University of Pittsburgh, David now calls Richmond, Virginia, home. The city is vibrant with arts and culture, which David considers an encouraging part of his library's mission. He lives proudly inside the city limits with his wife, children, and dogs. His coworkers and neighbors find him tolerable for a Yankee.